Technology Deals

Case Studies for
Officers, Directors,
Investors, and General Counsels
about
IPO's, Mergers, Acquisitions,
Venture Capital, Licensing,
Litigation, Settlements, Due Diligence
and
Patent Strategies

Stephen C. Glazier

Books by Stephen C. Glazier

Patent Strategies for Business
Third Edition

e-Patent Strategies
for
Software, e-Commerce, the Internet,
Telecom Services, Financial Services,
and Business Methods
(with Case Studies and Forecasts)

Technology Deals
Case Studies for
Officers, Directors,
Investors, and General Counsels
about
IPO's, Mergers, Acquisitions,
Venture Capital, Licensing,
Litigation, Settlements, Due Diligence
and
Patent Strategies

Technology Deals

Case Studies for
Officers, Directors,
Investors, and General Counsels
about
IPO's, Mergers, Acquisitions,
Venture Capital, Licensing,
Litigation, Settlements, Due Diligence
and
Patent Strategies

Companion Volume
to
Patent Strategies for Business
Third Edition
and
e-Patent Strategies

Stephen C. Glazier
Washington, D.C.

LBI Law and Business Institute
Washington, D.C.

Cataloging in Publication Data

Glazier, Stephen C.
        Technology Deals, Case Studies for Officers, Directors, Investors, and General Counsels about IPO's, Mergers, Acquisitions, Venture Capital, Licensing, Litigation, Settlements, Due Diligence and Patent Strategies/Stephen C. Glazier.
        Includes index.
        ISBN 0-9661437-5-2 (hardbound)
        ISBN 0-9661437-4-4 (paperback)
        1. Patents. 2. e-Commerce. 3. Software-Protection. 4. the Internet.
I. Title.

Library of Congress Control Number: 2004090013
ISBN: 0-9661437-5-2 (hardbound), ISBN 0-9661437-4-4 (paperback)

Printed variously in the United States of America and the U.K.
Hardbound. Paperback.

Contents

A. Case Studies

B. New Strategies for Technology Deals

About the Author

Stephen C. Glazier practices law in Washington, D.C., regarding patents, copyrights, trademarks, patent due diligence for M & A, patent demand letters and patent litigation, venture capital, licensing, the monetization of intellectual property, and related business transactions for technology companies. He has a B.S. and an M.S. from the Massachusetts Institute of Technology (M.I.T.), and a J.D. from the University of Texas. He is a member of the bar in New York, California, Texas, and the District of Columbia, and he is a registered patent attorney with the U.S. Patent and Trademark Office.

Mr. Glazier holds six U.S. patents, in which he invents around prior art patents, for clients. Mr. Glazier is the author of three books. He lectures frequently on legal and business topics, and is a contributor on current legal subjects to the editorial pages of *The Wall Street Journal* and other publications.

Mr. Glazier is a partner in the law firm of Kirkpatrick & Lockhart LLP, and is head of the Washington Patent Group of that firm. He may be contacted in Washington, D.C. at e-mail: glazier@alum.MIT.edu or sglazier@kl.com, telephone: 202-778-9000, fax: 202-778-9100.

Kirkpatrick & Lockhart LLP is a general practice law firm with about 750 attorneys in 10 offices, including about 50 patent attorneys. For more information, see www.kl.com.

Intellectual Property Equals Shareholder Value

"Technology is a differentiator in all markets."
-John Reed, former Chairman of Citibank

Intellectual property = shareholder value.

This equation is why this book was written. In today's economy, well developed intellectual property is as necessary to business success, and to a good stock price, as real estate and equipment have always been. Surprisingly, this is true of most business sectors, even those not traditionally thought of as "high tech" businesses. For example, even banks and insurance companies are developing patent portfolios to protect both the services that they sell, and the infrastructure that they use to sell and support those services.

IP = Shareholder Value

With the rise of intellectual property as a driver of shareholder value, the realization has followed that intellectual property is property. As such, it can be bought, sold, rented, and used as collateral, much as any other kind of property, such as real estate, equipment, or cash.

The criticality of intellectual property ("IP") in all markets, is an idea that came into its own in the 90's. In the beginning of the 90's, it was unusual for the IP attorneys to be called into large corporate transactions, and the financial community had little sensitivity to IP.

I remember working on a bridge financing in the early 90's for a technology company, to prepare for their IPO, and getting a call from a very large institutional venture capital ("VC") firm. The VC's were considering investing about $10 million. The first words out of their mouths were "we don't know much about patents, but we have some questions ... " They went on to ask questions making it clear that, indeed, they knew almost nothing about patents. Amazing. Real technology investing is largely a matter of buying an "investment grade patent portfolio", with a team to implement it; but obliviousness was the state of sensitivity (or, better said, insensitivity) to IP in the early 90's, among the financial community. *Stac Electronics v. Microsoft Corp.* , discussed herein, changed all that forever.

In the early 90's, I also had an academic interest in liens and security interests in IP. It was academic only because clients tended to have no interest at that time in the subject. It was not until 1992 that I first found client interest in this area of IP as collateral. A syndicate of European banks was making loans to U.S. software companies. The borrowers of course had no real assets, except IP, and the banks wanted the IP as collateral. The banks were incredulous that U.S. statutes were unclear about how to lien IP (the ambiguity in the statutes remain unchanged), but at least these banks were interested in using the technique.

But by the end of the 90's, all this had completely changed. Banks, venture capitalists, underwriters, and, indeed, the entire financial community had finally become patent sensitive. Now for almost any corporate deal, the quality of the subject intellectual property portfolio, and the status of the intellectual property strategy, are on the checklist of the financial parties.

It is today typical for a VC, or large company, when doing their due diligence for a possible funding or purchase of a smaller technology company, to ask if the products and services of the target are securely protected by patents and other intellectual property. In effect they are asking, "do we have to fund, or buy, these guys, or can we just copy their stuff for free?" Multi-million dollar deals are being accepted or rejected now based on an analysis of the target's intellectual property portfolio.

And from the point of view of the small technology company that would like to prepare itself for deals with VC's or a large buyer, it is essential that the little upstart develop an "investment grade intellectual property portfolio", that forces the answer to the preceding question to be favorable to the upstart. That is, does the Big Kahuna have to fund or buy the upstart, because no one can go around the upstart's IP? The upstart wants to force the answer to this question to be "yes". This is particularly true in software enabled technologies and services, since software can be relatively easy to reverse engineer and copy.

Since patents can now be used to own new services, in addition to the novel software that supports these new services, the new trend to patent 'everything under the sun' now even applies to many service industries, such as banking, investments, insurance, telecom services, entertainment, and medical service. For the first time, nimble players in these industries are now locking in competitive advantages for a generation, by developing key patent portfolios for services and software infrastructure. Banks are inventing!

And these developments are impacting the stock price of the companies involved. The enormity of this change was brought home to me recently when I read the latest 10-K annual report of an insurance company. This annual report discussed how the company's unique patent portfolio for insurance products and e-commerce infrastructure resulted in a PE ratio for its stock that was higher than the average for the insurance industry. "Intellectual property = shareholder value", even in the insurance and banking industries.

The change is huge and the rules have shifted forever.

Stephen C. Glazier
Washington, D.C.
1 March 2003

WHAT THE REVIEWERS ARE SAYING ABOUT THE COMPANION VOLUME

Patent Strategies
for
Business
Third Edition

"Stephen Glazier's book entitled *Patent Strategies for Business, Third Edition*, is a field manual for the intellectual property strategist to start thinking and acting... Glazier's book is one of the few sources which makes the effort to approach the patent field as a matter of strategy rather than as a matter of... how the authorities line up on each particular legal issue... Glazier's book lets the reader understand in a brief and manageable way how things work in the patent field... The writer wishes Glazier would convert his book into a multi-volume loose leaf series for which there is surely strong need and probably no better potential author or editor."

-Intellectual Property Rights News
Volume 2, Number 3
(Winter 1998)

TO OBTAIN THIS BOOK

It is easy to obtain a copy of this book, or either of its Companion Volumes: (1) *Patent Strategies for Business, Third Edition*, and (2) *e-Patent Strategies for Software, e-Commerce, the Internet, Telecom Services, Financial Services, and Business Methods (with Case Studies and Forecasts)*. All you have to do is one of the following:

(1) Go to the Web, to
        Amazon.com
        Barnesandnoble.com
        Booksamillion.com
        Amazon.co.uk
or to one of the many other book selling Web sites.

(2) See your bookstore. They may have the book in stock, and if not, they can order it for you.

(3) In the U.S., booksellers and libraries may contact their account representative at Ingram Book, or Baker & Taylor, or NACSCORP.

(4) In the U.K., booksellers and libraries may contact their account representative at Bertrams, or Gardners.

Acknowledgments

My clients over the years have pressed me to invent and organize the ideas found in this book. Ultimately, those clients gave these ideas their greatest seal of approval: they used them. I would like to give my clients, past and present, special thanks.

(However, my best ideas remain in my unpublished confidential correspondence with my clients.)

Hi, Hawkwood! Hi, Jody! Hi, Mom!

1

Patent Due Diligence For Financing Technology Companies: Case Studies

"I do not take business risks; I control them."
-J. P. Morgan

"Chance favors the well-informed."
-Marcel Proust

"My best ideas are somebody else's."
-Benjamin Franklin

Due diligence for intellectual property is becoming increasingly important in mergers and acquisitions, venture capital, IPO's (initial public offerings), and other financial transactions for technology companies. For technology company deals, patent due diligence can make or break a deal, or radically change the price.

This is due to several factors. One factor is the increased market capitalization of technology companies that have always viewed intellectual property, particularly patents, as critical to their market share and profit margins. These companies, including now software companies and Internet companies, are actively engaged in mergers and acquisitions. Also, the telecom world outside of the Internet is being changed by a combination of de-regulation, mergers and acquisitions, and a very dynamic technology infrastructure (including wireless, the Internet, convergence of cable and telephone, PCS, satellite-base wireless, and electronic commerce). Similar growth and M&A activity in the entertainment industry, where copyright of content and trademarks, are the crown jewels, have also brought intellectual property due diligence to M&A.

Another factor contributing to the importance of intellectual property due diligence in technology finance, is the increasing number of industries, some long established, that are newly coming to the patent world. In the United States, it has now been well established (in this decade) that software developments are patentable. Also, there is a new federal appeals case, *State Street Bank & Trust Co. v. Signature Financial Group, Inc*, 149 F.3rd 1368, 47 U.S.P.Q. 2d 1596 (Fed. Cir. 1998), that clarified that even software enabled financial services are patentable. Hence, now we have at least two new industries, financial services (including banks, securities brokerages, insurance companies, savings and loans, asset managers, program traders, mutual fund managers, and others) and telecom service providers (as opposed to telecom equipment manufacturers) that are moving actively into the patent arena for their software-enabled services. These are two large established industries with huge market capitalizations that are consolidating and reorganizing with extensive M&A activities, which have newly found themselves dealing with patent crown jewels for new market sectors.

Case studies from practice can be looked at to shed light on patent due diligence in corporate transactions. Lessons can be drawn from these practice examples about the best ways to pursue these activities. (As they say in the old black and white detective movies, the names have been changed to protect the innocent in some of these case studies. Where specific names of parties are mentioned, all the information given has been drawn from the public record, and no client relationship has existed between this author and the indicated parties.)

2

Case Study:
Due Diligence as
Industrial Espionage, or
"My Best Ideas Are
Somebody Else's"

Regardless of the original intent of the parties, any due diligence project can in retrospect appear to have worked like a sophisticated commercial espionage project against a competitor. This can be fine for the party that gains the information, if it violates no law and breached no contract. However, for the party that teaches in this process, it must be a no win game.

Take this scenario. Big Fish Co. expresses an interest in investing in, buying out, joint venturing with, or using as a supplier, the aspiring Mullet Co. Mullet Co. is of consider-able interest because it has developed a wonderful new fish hook early warning system, but does not have the capital to market it outside the metropolitan area of Pikes Peak, Colorado. But before Big Fish can make a decision on Mullet, Big Fish must do its due diligence and become an expert on Mullet and its product.

In the due diligence process, Mullet shows Big Fish its books, and the software algorithm that makes the hook alarm so unique and effective. Big Fish loves the algorithm, which is so brilliant that it requires only four lines of source code. But Big Fish walks the deal because its bylaws require that all members of the Board of Directors have a driver's license, and this disqualifies the President of Mullet Co., until he has two more birthdays. And Mullet Co. insists: no Board seat, no deal with Big Fish.

Six months later, Big Fish is on the market across the continent with a hook alarm that works almost as well as Mullet's and costs twice as much. But Mullet Co. is chopped into fish meal by Big Fish's huge sales force.

Was all this a sophisticated spying job by Big Fish, or an unavoidable development? After all, most prospective deals never happen. In fact, the answer to the question means little to the parties, except as it may affect their legal rights.

(But there is a happy ending for Mullet Co. Mullet has one of those new software patents for its algorithm, and sued Big Fish for patent infringement. To Big Fish's surprise, Mullet won and received a nine figure judgment and a permanent injunction against infringement. Big Fish starts shipping its hook alarms without software and sales crash. Within a week, Big Fish is back at the negotiating table with

Mullet. Mullet's founders sell out for a huge price, and they all go fishing.)

The tension in due diligence is that the cooperative target must treat due diligence as an actual espionage activity, but still try to get a friendly deal done. Non-disclosure agreements can be obtained, but they are only contracts that can be breached, and for which any defendant may have defenses. The Uniform Trade Secrets Act found in many states may give some recourse, if the aggrieved party survives. Also, the new federal *Economic Espionage Act of 1966* may give some relief. (See chapter 26 of   *Patent Strategies for Business, third edition*, the companion volume to this book, for a detailed discussion of this topic.) Perhaps the best course for the target is to reveal as little as possible, and reveal no technical product information at all that is not in pending or issued patents.

In the above scenario, if Big Fish is in fact using the Mullet algorithm, Mullet will be best protected if the algorithm is claimed in valid patents owned by Mullet. As Stac showed in its litigation discussed below, only this strategy can make Mullet a piranha, instead of chopped bait.

3

Case Study:
Stac v. Microsoft, or
"Are these Guys Protected?"

"6/08/94 --   *PERMANENT INJUNCTION [against future infringement] against defendant Microsoft Corp. ..*

6/13/94 --   *AMENDED JUDGMENT AND ORDER ... Microsoft shall pay Stac $120,000,000.00 ... "*
- Civil Docket for Case # 93-CV-413
Stac Electronics v. Microsoft Corp.

"PLEASE READ THIS NOTE CAREFULLY. MS-DOS 6.21, the version included with your new PC, does not include the DoubleSpace compression utility. The documentation you received includes references to the DoubleSpace feature. Please disregard any reference to DoubleSpace in the accompanying documentation. We apologize for any inconvenience this may cause you."

-    *From a sticker on the back of the MS-DOS 6.2 Manual, shipped after June 8, 1994. The "DOS Lobotomy by Stac" Notice.*

The preceding parable in Case No. 1 may show some relation to the fact pattern in *Stac Electronics v. Microsoft Corp.* (D.C. C. Cal. CV-93-413-ER, 1994). In this suit a small firm with a software patent (Stac Electronics, which had a patent on the algorithm for its PC hard disc data compression software product) defended its market niche in court against a large infringing corporation (Microsoft).

The lesson for the patent buyer, inventor, or underwriter, from *Stac Electronics* and the preceding case study above, is that the target must be carefully reviewed to ascertain if its products are adequately protected by intellectual property strategies. Only then can the target be protected from copying or reverse engineering.

The second lesson, from Big Fish's and Microsoft's point of view, is that a new product or service must be carefully reviewed to assure that it does not infringe a competitor's patent position.

Apparently, Microsoft had expressed an interest in working with Stac, and did due diligence on the Stac product. In this process, Microsoft apparently decided to copy the compression algorithm of the Stac product. Microsoft then wrote its own code to execute the Stac algorithm and used the code in the Microsoft DOS 6.2 product.

Stac sued Microsoft for patent infringement, copyright infringement, and trade secret violations. Stac lost on all counts except the patent infringement count, on which Stac won. Stac received a judgment of about $120 million, plus a permanent injunction against Microsoft to stop further infringement.

After the litigation, for about a week, a lobotomized version of DOS was shipped with the compression feature disabled. DOS manuals were shipped with stickers on the cover warning to ignore the chapter on compression, because the feature had been disabled (pursuant to the federal injunction). After about a week of this, Microsoft cut a deal with Stac by which Microsoft, apparently, paid Stac a large amount of cash, Microsoft made a large capital investment in Stac, and Microsoft received a license to use the algorithm in DOS.

Apparently, after getting caught in court by the patent, Microsoft thought it wanted to deal after all. And Stac found a price that looked good.

If not for its patent and the resulting injunction against Microsoft, Stac would likely be in serious financial trouble today, or out of business. How could Stac sell its product if the same features were available in DOS (or Windows 95) for free? Without a patent, Stac would have just been a free test market project for Microsoft.

Notice that Stac's corporate life was saved by its software patents only (which covered its basic algorithm). Software copyright got nothing for Stac because Microsoft did not copy source code; instead, Microsoft apparently just wrote new code for the same algorithm.

This is the new paradigm. This is how a little software company can save itself from annihilation by a giant with overwhelming market power and financial strength.

This approach also applies to any easily copied product or service that can be protected by software patents. Financial products and services are a prime example of this. New financial products are now receiving patent protection by a species of software patent. This is important because a new financial product can be very quickly copied once it achieves market success.

Immediately after Stac's courtroom victory against Microsoft, the president of Stac announced to the public, correctly we think, that this was the new paradigm for the development and marketing of new software developments. That is, patents must be obtained for new software products, so that they can be protected from easy copying and infringement.

Note that this patent protection for software is superior to the traditional copyright protection. This is because copyright protects little more than copying of source code, and perhaps screen displays and user interfaces, while patents can protect the basic concept of a software product, regardless of the actual source code. In the case of *Stac Electronics v. Microsoft Corp.*, Microsoft avoided a copyright problem but ran afoul of patents.

The further development of this new paradigm can be seen in the very recent initiation of further Internet software patent cases, including *Priceline.com v. Microsoft Corp.*,

Amazon.com v. Barnesandnoble.com, Trilogy v. Carsdirect.- com, and the Yahoo.com litigation. In each of these cases, freshly issued software e-commerce patents went straight to enforcement litigation. It is expected that many more such patents are in the application pipeline at the Patent Office, and will lead to further developments to be watched with great interest.

4

Case Study:
Own It Before You Sell It

Godzilla Corp. was a big corporation with about 900 engineers on its staff, business activities in several high tech areas, and no patent portfolio or technology spin off operations.

At some point, Godzilla's brain, its upper management that is, got the brilliant idea that 900 engineers employed in high tech fields may occasionally have a new idea of value. Godzilla smelled money. Furthermore, with over $20 billion in revenues, the Big Lizard (as its employees called it, affectionately we think) felt that it could scrape up a few bucks to chase a good business opportunity.

Leaping into the field in a big way, Godzilla selected one new gizmo, the Big Can, got the Lizard lawyers to apply for and receive a patent on it, and began marketing the opportunity.

The pitch was good: Godzilla needed the Big Can, but nobody made the Big Can, so Godzilla had to design and manufacture the Big Can for itself. Now all the other little lizards in the business also needed the Big Can, but Godzilla was not a manufacturer, at heart, but a consumer of Big Cans. Of course, nobody else could make the Big Can, even for their own use, because 'Zilly had the patent monopoly. Unless, of course, you did a license deal with the Lizard. License the patent, hire the Lizard engineers as consultants to teach you how to make the Big Can, and then you would be the Big Cheese of the Big Can. It would be easy. The testimonials alone from the Happy Lizard would sell the product.

Godzilla spent $750,000 marketing the pitch to the major players. They had a license deal cut with Not So Big Can Corp., a can company with ambitions to become, well, bigger. Not So Big would give Godzilla seven figures up front (that is, several million dollars), and a percentage of the gross, for the life of the patent. Godzilla's projections indicated about $100 million in royalties from the deal over the remaining life of the patent.

Godzilla was ready to party, the deal looked so good. The Liz was even considering filing another patent application (they still had 899 engineers left with untapped ideas).

After extensive negotiations, a huge and complicated license and joint venture agreement was negotiated between Lizard and Can. They were ready to sign, pass the check, and open the champagne.

Three days before the closing, Not So Big did some due diligence on Godzilla and the contract.

Stop the music.

The first thing Not So Big's intellectual property attorney did was to check title. That is, he checked the records to see who owned the $100 million patent in question. Whoops, no assignment was on file for that patent in the public patent assignment records. The legal details are involved, but basically Godzilla needed a written assignment for the patent from the individual named inventor to Godzilla (even though the inventor was an employee of Godzilla), for the $100 million deal to close. Now, Not So Big is in the business of making deals, not breaking deals. And the point of finding title defects is not to kill a deal, but to correct the defect before it kills the deal maker.

They tell me that the meeting with Godzilla and the inventor was rather ugly. At first, the inventor held out for too much money, so much that it would have killed the deal. Finally, the inventor settled for a large cash "early retirement" package, and signed the assignment to Godzilla. The deal was saved, barely, at considerable extra expense.

I am sure that on the next deal, Godzilla will save a lot of money, and very likely save the deal, by checking title to its patent before it develops and markets the product. I have found that an employee or consultant will usually sign away rights to intellectual property, on the front end, in order to initiate or maintain employment. However, on the back-end, after they see a big market developing, their hand can get paralysis. Feeding their checking account appears, at that point, to be the only cure for this strange disease.

5

Case Study:
Buying the Defendant's Seat?

Strip Co. had a machine that manufactured a particular part with a plastic strip laminated on it that could record information. Strip Co. wanted to sell this product line to concentrate on other lines of business. Strip Co. contacted Large Co., which was interested in making machines that made parts with plastic memory strips . The parties negotiated a contract providing for the sale "the product line" for a $15 million one-time cash payment. Strip Co. had a patent portfolio of six U.S. patents that covered its "product line", provisions for assignments of which were included in the contract. Three days before the closing, Large Co. started a bit of patent due diligence.

Initially the Large Co. patent attorney had difficulty in translating "a product line" into any species of legal property. That is, the contract appeared vague as to the description of a fundamental term, that is, the goods or property being sold. Since the machinery in question was manufactured by Strip

Co. only to order, no inventory was maintained. There was one purchase order for which equipment was being manufactured, so that the rights in that executory contract could be assigned together with the work in progress for that purchase order. Other than that, no property to be transferred could be identified other than the portfolio of six patents.

That then, a patent portfolio, was largely what Large Co. was really buying.

Considering the three day deadline for closing, Large Co. immediately checked title for the six patents. Counsel found that written assignments had been filed at the Patent Office by the inventor of record to his employer, Strip Co. only in the case of four patents. That is, the two other patents in the portfolio, according to the public assignment records, still remained the property of the individual named inventors, and not of Strip Co. That is, Strip Co. was endeavoring to sell the property for which there was a title defect, to put the matter optimistically.

In the interest of making deals rather that breaking deals, Large Co. demanded that the contract be amended to include (1) a covenant to convey title to the patent portfolio, (2) representations and warranties of good and unencumbered title to the patent portfolio, and non-infringement by the Strip Co. products of the patents of competition, and (3) various other representations and warranties. Furthermore, Large Co. demanded that the entire payment of the purchase price be placed in escrow pending verification of the representations and warranties, and performance of the covenants. The closing in three days would in effect be a conditional closing with the funds escrowed pending verification of title, non-infringement and other points. After much noise by Strip Co., the escrow of the purchase price was established.

Further activity during the escrow determined that the inventors of one of the "loose" patents were American citizens and residents, and still in the employ of Strip Co. Their assignments were obtained quickly and without incident (but it is not generally known at what cost).

However, the inventor and owner of record of the sixth patent was a Japanese citizen and resident, who at the time of the sale had advanced to the somewhat distant relationship with Strip Co., of being an ex-employee. Indeed, the inventor had retired and was thought to have moved to the northern Japanese island of Hokkaido. No current information was immediately available as to where (or whether) he still lived. After several months Strip Co. did produce an assignment to Strip Co. in English of all rights in the Japanese inventor's patent, with a Japanese signature and notarization.

During this extended escrow period while the assignment from Japan was being obtained by Strip Co., further due diligence was undertaken.

One aspect of the due diligence project was to obtain and review the major prior art patents related to Strip Co.'s patents. General first impressions of validity were obtained from this analysis.

Also, Large Co.'s patent counsel stepped back and looked at the body of the prior art to make general characterizations of the portfolio as it may appear useful to the transaction in any manner. It was determined that the prior art patents by competitors probably suggested the range of competing products in the marketplace. The prior art patents were grouped according to their owners, and it was concluded that the most significant portfolios of prior art owned by competitors were in fact owned by the two largest competitors of Strip Co. Furthermore, it was determined that there was a substantial possibility that the products represented by Strip Co.'s patent portfolio may be dominated by the patent portfolios of prior art owned by Strip Co.'s largest competitor.

That is, on the face of the patents analyzed, it appeared that if Strip Co. in fact manufactured and sold the products claimed in Strip Co.'s own patent portfolio, then Strip Co. may run a substantial chance of infringing the earlier prior art patent portfolio of its major competitor. That is, a major motivation for Strip Co. selling its product line at this time may be to avoid a possible infringement suit by its major competitor.

Large Co. determined to proceed with the acquisition, but as a result of the due diligence and the identified risk of infringement, the purchase price was discounted from $15 million in cash to $7 million, with $3 million paid in cash at closing and $4 million paid over time, provided that no infringement claims arose.

Hence, the patent due diligence on this project succeeded in closing the transaction, but points identified regarding title defects, patent coverage and potential infringement led to a material modification in the price terms and the general business evaluation of the acquisition target.

The lesson here for the seller is to clean up your patent portfolio, to raise it to investment grade, before the deal. If you can.

For the buyer, a tactical lesson here is that the earlier you do the due diligence, the better. And look at title first.

A strategic lesson here, for the buyer, is that patent due diligence can have a multi-million dollar impact on the price and terms of an acquisition, even after the original term sheet has been agreed to. Your patent lawyer, if he can cut a deal with what he knows, can be a critical member of the acquisition team. Furthermore, patent due diligence can result in a target of greater eventual value. That is, your patent attorney can identify a plan to increase the shareholder value of the target (a plan not necessarily shared with the target before the closing). In other words, your patent lawyer at the deal table can help you spend less money to buy a more valuable company. Get more for less – that is a nice goal in the mergers and acquisitions market.

6

Case Study:
Patent What You Sell,
Sell What You Patent

Needles Co. had a line of medical devices that had
been developed by its founder and CEO, Mr. Needles. Mr.
Needles was approaching his late fifties and wanted to sell his
company, and spend the remainder of his career developing
products for manufacture and sale by others. Needles Co. was
headquartered in Australia but had sales throughout the world,
with its biggest single market in the United States. Needles
Co. approached a large U.S. medical device company, Big
Medco, which liked its products. However, the evaluation
was that Mr. Needles had little to sell other than the customer
list of Needles Co. since none of the products were protected
by patents. Big Medco could simply copy the devices of
Needles Co. and manufacture without royalty payment.

At this point Mr. Needles went to U.S. patent counsel
to seek a remedy. U.S. patent counsel determined that the

devices currently on sale by Needles Co. could not be patented in the U.S. because they had been on sale for more than one year. However, the strategy was developed to immediately patent all products currently under development by Needles Co., and to aggressively pursue second generation improvements to the current product line where such improvements could themselves be patentable. Hopefully, then the current product line in the public domain could be made obsolete and replaced by second generation improvements that were patented and proprietary to Needles Co.

In this way it was hoped that Needles Co. could evolve from a public domain manufacturer to a proprietary patented manufacturer. This would then require Big Medco to buy Needles Co. on the basis of a multiple of its earnings, rather than simply for the value of its customer list.

Over the next six years a portfolio of U.S. patents and foreign counterpart patents were obtained by Needles Co. for over a dozen of its main products. Most of the patents were invented by Mr. Needles himself. In some instances, patent counsel co-invented certain improvements for the benefit of Needles Co., in what might be called, "legally driven" product development. (That is, product development and patenting driven by legal analysis of patentability opportunities developed from the related patent prior art. Traditionally, there are two approaches to new product development, "market driven" and "technology driven". "Legally driven" product development is a third possible approach to product development and innovation that is new and relatively unknown, but can be highly productive).

Furthermore, the developing patent portfolio of Needles Co. became a growing prior art bar to the later patent applications of Needles Co. itself. In response to this expected and natural trend, the patent applications of Needles Co. began to incorporate more and more software novelty, rather than merely hardware novelty. This coincided with the general trend towards "smart" medical equipment that developed parallel with the legal developments in the United States allowing for the patentability of software. Although a "medical device company", the highest profit margins for Needles Co. now came from sales of its patented software, and of unpatentable disposable parts needed in each use of the software.

While developing this patent portfolio, Needles Co. added to its proprietary product line by going public in Australia and acquiring (for stock) a competitor located in Italy with a patented product line. At the end of last year, Mr. Needles reapproached Big Medco and sold Needles Co. in a transaction for stock and cash, and at a valuation that was a material premium over the then publicly trading price for Needles Co. In his last communication with U.S. patent counsel, Mr. Needles informed counsel that he was purchasing a new house, rumored to be one of the largest private residences in Australia.

A lesson here is "everyone is a software company now".

Another lesson here is "sell what you can patent and patent what you can sell".

For the buyer, the due diligence lesson is to carefully review the products <u>and the software</u> for patentability. For the seller, the lesson is the same, but do it well in advance to develop an investment grade intellectual property portfolio.

7

Case Study:
Buying and Selling
(Intellectual) Property,
Monetizing Intellectual Property

There are several possible goals for an intellectual property ("IP") development program. They may include facilitating financing, legitimately restraining competitors from entering your market niche, or generating revenues from licensing. Sometimes, however, changing business strategies and circumstances lead a company to unintentionally own a legacy patent portfolio that is not applicable to any currently planned product line. At that point, however, a write off of the intellectual property investment is not necessarily required. Instead, IP may be sellable to another entity. It may even be a home run profit center in itself.

Take this case. ClickCo (this is a pseudonym, although in today's market it may not be readily apparent) was a zippy little startup with four employees, including the founder, in the 90's. They had big plans and a sparkling business plan to develop certain cool algorithms to be used in wireless widgets. The algorithms could be hardwired or compact software engines.

Wireless widgets were hot with the venture capital community that month, and the Clicksters obtained about $5 million in first round funding. ClickCo developed some very interesting designs for wireless widget pieces, with software for particularly efficient algorithms. On advice of their venture capitalists, ClickCo invested money in a patent portfolio for the distinctive software algorithms for their wireless widgets and obtained a half dozen U.S. patents for these devices.

These software patent applications were somewhat controversial because they were filed at the U.S. Patent Office before the <u>In Re Alappat</u> case, before the promulgation of the guidelines for software inventions by the U.S. Patent Office ("the Alappat Guidelines"), and before the surrender of the U.S. Patent Office in its legal struggle against allowing software patents. However, ClickCo 's technology attorney was convinced that the law was moving in a pro-software patent direction and there was adequate legal precedence to file these early software applications. Indeed, he felt that early priority dates were essential in this fast moving telecom software area.

Eventually ClickCo developed a unit of six design engineers employed on this project to develop the wonderful wireless widgets.

The manufacturing industry for wonderful wireless widgets consolidated at a very rapid pace. Eventually, the three or four major players in the wonderful wireless widget market obtained tremendous economies of scale, and it became clear that a new entrant into the manufacture of wonderful wireless widgets, even with superior technology, could never make it up the steep economies of scale curve in time to compete adequately with the four earlier first-out manufacturers.

Under some duress from their venture capitalists, the engineers at ClickCo determined to terminate the pursuit of the wireless widget market and place their bets on a new developing industry, involving pseudo analog non-computer communication over TCP/IP protocols. (That worked out to be a wonderful bet, but that is another case.)

This new bet on the TCP/IP protocols left ClickCo with an inherited legacy portfolio and engineering team in the wireless widget world. It was a wonderful wireless widget, but is was a no longer fit with the Clicky strategy.

Rather than writing off the intellectual property investment in the wireless widget, and administering organizational euthanasia to the engineering design team, ClickCo decided that they may be able to sell the legacy widget patent portfolio, and the related widget designs protected by the IP portfolio, together with the engineering team, to one of the huge consolidated players that would remain in the wireless widget world. (Without the patent piece, the package would not be worth much; it is hard to sell design ideas that buyers, and competitors can copy for free.) ClickCo would in effect become a royalty owner or a recipient of a one-time prepaid up front royalty. ClickCo had superior technology in the wireless widget world, they just did not have a market opportunity that would admit a new manufacturing entrant, even with superior technology. However, an existing player in the manufacturing field with economies of scale might be able to exploit their great new technology. In fact, ClickCo decided that instead of just amputating the gangrenous limb, they would cut if off and sell it as transplant material to another business body. If you can't beat them, sell out to them at a profit.

At the same time, the ClickCo TCP/IP software products were booming. ClickCo faced the irony of successful growth companies. Their exploding sales provided tremendous income, but as their working capital expanded they actually had negative cash flow. In cases of acute success, booming income equals negative cash flow. All that profit was killing them. ClickCo needed a large capital infusion. To do this, ClickCo was planning a $10 million third tier private placement to prepare for a follow on IPO in about a year. The $10 million IPO would represent a substantial dilution of the equity of the shareholders of ClickCo.

At this point, ClickCo obtained a buyer of its widget IP portfolio, and a future employer of the six design engineers in question. The overall payments from the deal, assuming certain sales figures were hit and benchmarks met after sale, would total approximately $40 million over two years. As it turned out, this would avoid the need for any third round private placement (and dilution of shareholders) and permit an IPO on schedule in a year without further prior dilution.

Furthermore, since only $10 million in working capital was budgeted to get to the IPO and $40 million would be provided by the flip of the legacy patent portfolio, ClickCo actually ended up with more capital than it had originally required.

This extra capital allowed ClickCo to take advantage of an opportunity to acquire a large patent portfolio from an erstwhile competitor. This was of great value to the TCP/IP strategy of ClickCo, but the patents were of no further use to competitor. (Talk about a change of business plan: the competitor had been heavily invested in its main line of business, Buggywhips.com, which had tanked the company into a Chapter 11 liquidation. The TCP/IP product line was not the cause of death, and was a relatively minor line of this large company. However, you cannot take half a bath, and you cannot do half a bankruptcy, and the whole company went into the tank.) ClickCo bought the TCP/IP patents from the trustee in bankruptcy, for a substantial discount on what might have been their value if the seller were still in business.

The overarching lesson in this parable is that there are several alternative uses for an intellectual property portfolio. And if in the 20 year life of a patent portfolio, business circumstances and strategies change to make the original strategy of a segment of the patent portfolio inapplicable, then the patents may still turn to cash by pursuing one of the alternative strategic goals for intellectual property. Most of all, intellectual property is property and it can be sold to whoever may need it the most.

The current buzzword of using intellectual property as a source of income or capital, instead of simply holding it to enforce it against competitors and keep them out of a proprietary marketplace, is called "monetization". The origin of this usage is that it is the process of turning intellectual property into "money". This is not the meaning of monetization that Alan Greenspan or any traditional economist might have in mind, but it gets the point across on behalf of the bottom line.

8

Case Study: X-treme Rush Procedures for Patent Portfolio Development

Internet business moves at the speed of light, as they say. Consequently, we have found it necessary to develop unorthodox procedures for patent applications directed to e-commerce, GUI's, and related software. These expedited procedures for patent portfolio development, which are ethical and of nominal additional cost, accelerate the application review process at the PTO, and result in broader patents issued sooner. Clients appreciate these procedures when they "absolutely, positively" must get their patents allowed in a hurry. The following case study illustrates the procedure.

Faux Photon Inc. was a start-up dot com with an exciting new software-enabled Internet service that allowed it to quickly convert from an Internet service provider (ISP) to an application service provider (ASP). Faux needed an issued patent as soon possible, for four reasons: (1) Faux had identified an infringer, and the longer that Faux waited to take action the greater would become the infringer's market share and name recognition. (2) Faux had procured a license with a strategic partner to develop the invention in another market niche, and the license provided that Faux's royalty rate would double when its patent issued. (3) The PTO has demonstrated a tendency to perform a new prior art search each time they issue a new office action. The sooner the patent was allowed, therefore, the fewer searches the PTO would perform. Accordingly, the issued claims would likely be broader if issued sooner. (4) Faux was looking for a second round of funding. One large venture capitalist was interested, but very sensitive to proprietary issues. They would fund only after a patent issued.

Thus, Faux's patent counsel activated the following extreme (be cool, call it X-treme) rush procedure. It is not the normal way of doing things, but the Internet is not a normal market.

- File the first draft as a provisional application. As usual, patent counsel distributed the first draft of the patent application to the inventors for their review and comment. But because this iteration and drafting cycle takes time, the first draft was filed as a provisional at the same time that it was sent to the inventors for review. (The comments were incorporated into the later-filed regular application.)

- File in triplicate. Patent applications are assigned by lottery to examiners, some of whom are quite good and some horrible. So when the regular application was ready, Faux filed three substantively identical applications, except that each had a different title, abstract and field of search, and the claims were reordered so that each had a different claim 1 with a different species. As expected, this resulted in the three applications being assigned to three different examiners in three different art units. Faux waited to see which of the three examiners proved most competent and issued the most favorable first office action. Faux proceeded with that application and abandoned the other two. (Faux also cross-filed any examiner search results from the abandon applications into the application that continued to issuance.)

- File a petition to make special (to expedite review). The petition was not based on the conventional grounds, such as that the inventor was ill or the invention involved a cure for AIDS. Instead, it was based on the fact that a prior art search was filed along with the application, an under-appreciated basis for a petition to make special. (Typically, petitions to make special are not filed because it is an additional expense and the time to issuance is not so critical.)

- File "kitchen sink" claims (also called "Steve-o" claims) for each independent claim family. A kitchen sink claim is an special long independent claim that includes all of the limitations of a normal independent claim plus all of the limitations of the claims depending from that normal independent claim. This triggers the "one hand rule," which encourages the examiner to allow at least the kitchen sink claims in the initial office action. It also allows prosecution to begin with a "Yes" from the examiner rather than a "No." Subsequent negotiations then deal with how much more "Yes" the application will receive. (An application that begins with a "No" must first convert the "No" to a "Yes," before negotiating further "Yes's.")

- Request an examiner interview. Faux's patent counsel filed a letter with the original application requesting an examiner telephone interview prior to the first office action, and a personal interview in light of the urgency of the application and the petition to make special. In addition to the letter, prior to the first office action, Faux's patent counsel telephoned the examiner and re-requested an interview in order to explain the application.

- Accept immediately any early-allowed narrow patent, but file continuation applications for broader claims. The first office action resulted in allowance of the kitchen sink claims. Faux elected to receive a fast patent on only these claims and immediately paid the issue fee. Faux also filed a continuation application to prosecute the remaining claims, and again filed a petition to make special. Using the issued patent (with the narrower claims), Faux initiated infringement litigation against its target competitor. Later, when the broader claims in a continuation application issued, Faux added them to an amended complaint. Faux also got an immediate bump up in the royalty for its patent license and proceeded with its venture funding.

- Pursue submarine strategy. The submarine patent strategy lives, even though it now has a finite life. To wit, Faux filed an additional continuation application, without expediting it. This gave it the option of targeting claims to the competitor's specific products as they gradually appeared. Accordingly, Faux developed an active unit to monitor its competitors' patent activities and product releases, and to actively design around the competition's new patents and products.

Any patentee may consider these procedures when time is of the essence. As patents become increasingly important in the Internet world, these unorthodox extreme rush procedures may become the norm.

9

Case Study:
Your Software Consultant
or Your Competitor?

It used to be that software consultants would sign just about any contract for a nice software project. Things have changed. Software consultants are increasingly trying to develop proprietary software products out of their consulting practices. This has led to some intense negotiation over intellectual property ownership rights in software "consulting" contracts. Some of these negotiations are not very candid.

Here is a case that we lived through recently that illustrates the point. Lotsa Photon, Inc. developed a great idea for a new software system to address a major problem. In fact, this was a problem that was pandemic in their industry and Lotsa anticipated that their unique solution would give them a competitive advantage in the business. Lotsa developed a very specific RFP (Request for Proposal) with about

80 pages of specific performance requirements for a software package. They released this RFP on a confidential basis to five software houses that could write and de-bug the source code to get the system up and running.

XYZ Wiz Kid Consulting Company was picked as the favorite house to write and de-bug the source code to implement the Lotsa concept. On the front end, Lotsa made it clear that their strategy in developing this product was to capture a competitive advantage in the industry against their competitors. Consequently, Lotsa required that the Wiz Kid Consulting Company not provide a competing product to the industry, based on what they learned from Lotsa, and that Lotsa retain all intellectual property ownership rights to the concept and the product. XYZ Wiz Kid agreed to these terms, sniffing out a $5 million project to write the source code and install it. Detailed negotiations were commenced.

The Lotsa IP licensing attorney was surprised to find that the proposed draft of the consulting agreement delivered by XYZ Wiz Kid had an annoying provision buried on page 37 in a parenthetical sub-clause. This fine print provided that XYZ Wiz Kid would retain any patent rights, copyrights, or other intellectual property in the source code that XYZ Wiz Kids wrote, but that Lotsa would have a paid up perpetual non-exclusive, non-assignable license to operate the product in its facilities.

Since this provision from XYZ Wiz Kid would allow the Wiz Kids to sell cloned copies of the software development to competitors of Lotsa, Lotsa required that XYZ Wiz

Kid remove this "erroneous" provision from the draft contract. The Wiz Kids agreed.

However, the new draft of the proposed consulting agreement from Wiz Kid removed the provision from page 37, but an identical new provision was found by Lotsa on page 93. Surprise!

At this point, Lotsa's IP licensing counsel got particularly suspicious. He searched the European Patent Office for recently published patent applications in Munich by the Wiz Kids. Guess what? The Wiz Kids, while claiming no interest in the intellectual property rights of the software package, but while trying to trick Lotsa by inserting provisions to the contrary in the contract, had simultaneously applied for a software patent for the Lotsa development in Europe, claiming priority from an earlier filed U.S. Application by Wiz Kid for the same project. What the Wiz Kids had done was take the Lotsa confidential RFP, copy the ideas, write up a patent application based on it, and file it in the U.S. Patent Office under oath claiming that the Wiz Kids had invented the idea. Double Surprise!

At this point, Lotsa broke off negotiations with Wiz Kid and entered into a relationship with a competing software vendor. Reverse Surprise!

XYZ Wiz Kids had adopted a business plan in which their "clients" paid the Wiz Kids to develop products that the Wiz Kids could then own and resell freely to their clients' competitors.

Case Study: Consultant or Competitor?
43

What happened to the possible situation of Lotsa "infringing" its own invention as claimed in the Wiz Kids U.S. patent? No problem. Lotsa's patent attorney, in a fit of creative paranoia, had refused to let Lotsa release its RFP until he wrote up Lotsa's own patent application, based on the RFP, and filed it. The Lotsa U.S. patent application for the software development was filed about a week before the RFP was released, and about a month before the Wiz Kids "copy-cat" patent application was filed at the U.S. Patent Office. The Wiz Kids did not know it, but they were cut off at the PTO. Double reverse Surprise! As Lotsa's patent counsel said, "just because I am paranoid doesn't mean nobody is out to get us".

XYZ Wiz Kid's business plan makes a lot of sense for software consultants, and it sometimes makes sense for software consulting clients. However, it should be pursued in a more candid manner between client and consultant than in this case study.

This was done candidly and successfully in the classic case of Microsoft. Microsoft started life as a software consulting company. Then IBM hired Microsoft to develop DOS, but knowingly agreed that Microsoft could retain the rights of DOS after providing a license to IBM for the product. (It made sense at the time for both parties.) This deal is the basic foundation of the Microsoft empire.

This basic story of Microsoft, converting from a software consultant to a proprietary software company, is well known now and perhaps has inspired the major software consultants to follow the same route where possible.

This plan can often be pursued on a consensual basis between software consultants and a client on terms that are mutually attractive.

Indeed, today we see many companies and divisions, that were in the past purely software consultant businesses, that are now developing patent portfolios for proprietary software products.

This is a business plan that any software consulting company should consider. It is also a possibility that any client of a software consulting company should seriously review in their contract negotiations, to make sure that it does not happen contrary to the client's own intentions.

10

Case Study:
Web Page Deals,
Finding the New Property
in the New Economy

In the New Economy, deals sometime require a hunt for new forms of New Property.

Endless, Inc. had been in business a long time churning out large volumes of content. This included primarily content printed on paper, which Endless sold by the truckload, and other content on video clips. Being a traditional content publisher and generator, Endless had no activity on the Internet or Web.

WayCool.com, LLC developed a deal with Endless in which WayCool would obtain all the Web distribution rights for Endless content, for WayCool's planned new Web Site. The deal would include all rights necessary from Endless to make an Endless content Web site owned and operated by

WayCool. WayCool would pay Endless money up front, and a percentage of the revenues, and Endless would obtain an equity interest in WayCool. WayCool had obtained financing in a private placement to enable the first stage of the business. The race was on to document and close the transaction and come to a final agreement on the details of the Endless/Cool deal.

An interesting provision of the transaction that was still open was a "fine point". Would Endless' rights be sold unconditionally to WayCool in return for WayCool equity, or would WayCool grant a lien to Endless on Endless' rights, to secure certain performance targets by WayCool. In the latter case with the lien, if WayCool under performed. Then Endless could take back its rights and try its strategy of commercialization on the Web in a different vehicle. In the alternative without the security interest, if WayCool failed, then Endless' rights would remain in WayCool's shell, as would any other assets of WayCool. An alternative possibility for the transfer of rights would be a license from Endless to WayCool, which would be contingent upon continuing payment of royalties and other compensation.

One question for IP counsel at this point was: what is the property involved in a content deal for a Web Page? WayCool had the rights to use the Endless name on the Web Page, and to Endless content, and would receive the existing but underutilized non-commercial Web Page and domain name registration of Endless.

Regarding content, the deal looked like a conventional copyright transaction. Traditional copyright law well covers property rights and content, including print, video, audio, and other media. Also, the copyright statute, regarding liens, the perfection of liens and the foreclosure of the same, has a fairly well developed degree of specificity. However, there is an annoying and unnecessary statutory ambiguity in the method to protect and foreclose security interests in copyright. Particularly, the federal copyright statute has some provisions on these points, but it is unclear as to what extent they may or may not preempt all or part of state UCC law, which also claims jurisdiction. Unfortunately, the leading case which seems to be followed by most informed practice, *In re Peregrine*, is merely a federal district court case, and hence not from a dispositive forum.

Likewise, trademark law would cover the use by WayCool of the Endless name for WayCool's Web Site. However, the trademark statute has much the same incompleteness and ambiguity regarding perfection and foreclosure of security interests as the copyrights statute, except that the trademark statute is worse.

Liens are attempted to be granted and foreclosed increasingly in copyrights and trademarks, however, the uncertainty of the law in this area leaves much to be desired and is inferior to the level of lien and mortgage practice found in other species of property with more complete statutes, such as real estate, equipment, and other tangible forms of personal property.

The situation regarding what property may be represented by the domain name registration itself, unfortunately, is even more complicated and interesting. Domain names often incorporate trademarks and, hence, to have rights to use and operate such a domain name, one also needs the rights to the trade name incorporated in the domain name. This may be acquired by a license or assignment. A license of a trademark would require quality control of the Web page by the licensor of the mark, and is probably unacceptable to many licensees. Monitoring and quality control of licensees probably also is not of any interest to many licensors.

The trademark rights manifested in the domain name registration may also be assigned, but such an assignment must accompany sale or assignment of the business associated with the Web Page in the name.

The matter of the domain name registration itself, aside from the trademark that it may manifest, is a more interesting question, and an even more unsatisfactory legal situation for the owners. It is simply unclear at this point what species of property, if any, domain name purposes unrelated to ownership, the domain name is a contractual right between the registrant and the registrar. If this were the case for all purposes, then the rights in the registration contract could be assigned, and the perfected security interest could be perfected and foreclosed pursuant to the UCC. Many commentators are at a loss to determine what property domain name registration would entail, if not a contractual right between the registrant and registrar.

In this regard, it is interesting to note that the domain name assignment document available from NSI (Network Solutions, Inc.), the leading domain registrar in the United States, is often used as a property assignment document for the domain name registration. However, the fine print on this document itself indicates that its execution and recording with NSI does not affect or change the legal title to the domain name (even though this seems to be at odds with the title of the document).

In this context, then, how can WayCool execute due diligence on the property it is to receive, receive title of that property, and give a perfected security interest in the property back to the seller, Endless?

Because of the bad state of the federal statutes for patents, copyrights, and trademarks, authoritative title searches for these properties can not be made (that is, an unrecorded, and hence unsearchable, title document can be effective as to a bona fide purchaser without notice), and therefore, no title insurance or unqualified title opinions for these properties can be had. Congress could correct this situation easily, but has not.

The basic answer is that prophylactic practice can be pursued as best as possible, that such prophylactic practice is not necessarily common practice, and that the deal can be done. However, the transaction will have far less legal certainty than other transactions, such as in real estate and personal property, that are clearly within the regime of a complete and well written statute. Generally speaking, in the future we can expect an inordinate amount of litigation over ambiguities in these web deals, especially where they turn sour for business reasons, and a wave of such litigation can be expected in the next recession.

In this case, WayCool's star studded legal staff did several things to review title. They did conventional UCC searches in the state and county of residence of the seller, Endless, looking for liens on copyrights, trademarks, Web pages, and general intangibles (which in the terms of the UCC, if it applies at all, may extend to intellectual property). Furthermore, the assignment records of the Copyright Office were reviewed for possible assignments and security interests and mortgages in the copyright. Also, the Assignment Division of the Trademark Office and the Patent Office were reviewed for possible assignments, liens, and mortgages for trademark properties and any possible patents that may have been asserted by Endless for its Web page.

Furthermore, regarding the domain name registration, and UCC records searches were done in Northern Virginia and at the Secretary of State in the State of Virginia, in the situs of NSI as the domain name registrant.

The basic approach here is that where it is unclear whether the state or federal law applies in any and all title issues, a parallel course was run under each regime, the UCC and the federal regime.

Likewise, for purposes of closing title, assignments were filed for copyright in the Copyright Office, and for trademark in the Trademark Office. There were no patents to Assign in the Patent Office. And a Bill of Sale was obtained for the domain name contract right (a UCC general intangible).

In the case of an eventual foreclosure of the security interest, the case is even more unclear. It is difficult to do a foreclosure sale twice in alternative regimes to follow alternative possible procedures. Most particularly under the UCC, it is unclear what a Section 9-504 reasonable commercial sale would require procedurally for copyrights, trademarks, or a domain name registrations.

The bottom line on these new economy Web deals is that they can be done, but only with a degree of ambiguity and uncertainty regarding title that is unprecedented in any other species of property. This places a premium on creative lawyering, to minimize these risks, and to predict where the law is going on various new legal questions. In this way, profits on the deals can be maximized.

11

The New Intellectual Property Strategy for Officers and Directors

The old intellectual property strategy used to be merely "innovate or die". This is dead. It not adequate anymore. Unprotected innovation is merely a great help to your competitors. You become a free test market and R&D department for your competitors if you do unprotected innovation. You must innovate, then own it, then exploit it to turn it all to cash or market advantage.

Call this new strategy "create, own, exploit".

What Keeps CEO's Up at Night

Traditional barriers to entry that protected innovation are eroding. It is now necessary to protect innovation in some additional way, that is, with intellectual property rights, since innovation no longer enjoys the traditional barriers to entry against copiers and pirates.

Free entry to competitors to your markets; this is the CEO's nightmare.

The four classic barriers to competitive entry are:

1. Capital formation.

2. Recruiting and retention of key employees.

3. Proprietary distribution systems.

4. Proprietary supply relationships.

The Internet and global venture capital upsets these four old barriers to entry and crumbles them. It is now much easier with the Internet and global venture capital to enter any competitor's market place, as a start-up or a lateral competitor. Investment money is available. Employees are mobile. Distribution and supply systems on the Internet are cheap, global and wide open to any neophyte.

The New Barriers

Fortunately, patents and related Intellectual Property can protect critical products, services, and infrastructure, including software, Internet infrastructure, and delivery systems. This can protect both what is sold (goods and services), and how it is sold (special infrastructure).

Once patent protection is obtained, then brand protection may also be obtained with trademarks.

This double barrel approach of (1) patent protecting the current technologies and features of good, services, and infrastructure, and then (2) brand protecting them when trademarks, constitutes sustainable business advantage. These are the new primary barriers to entry to your markets by your competitors.

Note that John Reed, former Chairman and CEO at Citibank is a MIT business school graduate. He felt that "technology is a differentiator in all marketplaces." He was innovative as President of Citicorp and he thought, even in a traditionally no–tech or low-tech industry like banking, that technology was an important differentiator in the marketplace. He was very forward looking in obtaining patent protection for software driven services and infrastructure for Citibank. The Citibank group now has about 70 issued business method patents and the largest market cap in the S&P 500.

The new historic shift in shareholder value from the old economy to the new economy is from about 75% tangible assets and 25% intangible assets, to about 25% tangible assets and 75% intangible assets, according to a recent study by the Brookings Institute. To put it another way, Microsoft does not own much besides intellectual property in software that is otherwise easily copied. Yet, Microsoft has one of the largest market caps in the S&P 500.

Patent Leverage

One way to leverage is to license intellectual property. IBM collected about $1.5 billion in patent license revenue last year.

The other way to leverage is with injunctions. See Amazon.com v. Barnes and Noble.com. Injunctions are a CEO issue. This is true because junctions are a court order to get out of a particular line of business or infrastructure investment.

Joint ventures and acquisitions are increasingly designed specifically to beat the patent problem. See for example the Via joint venture with S3 to use the S3 patent portfolio to beat the competitors.

Also see the IBM/Dell computer deal. This is worth $16 billion to Dell and it is patent driven. In the IBM/Dell deal, IBM did a component sales deal with Dell because Dell had a patent exposure to IBM for chips bought by Dell from others. There are no royalties involved to IBM for patent licensing, however, IBM sold product to Dell that Dell would not otherwise have bought, and knocked out Dell's existing suppliers. That is, IBM used its patent portfolio to force increased sales to Dell as an alternative to patent infringement litigation.

There are also now patent and licensing pure plays in public stocks. See Rambus, Qualcomm and Alza. These are in computers, mobile phones, and pharmaceuticals, respectively.

Also see the Gem Star patent leverage strategy. Gem Star leverages patents to buy the corporations that they want to buy. The basic pitch is "you have a lot of exposure for patent infringement to us, so why don't you just sell out to us at a nice price and forget the litigation". That is, Gem Star is driving its M&A by buying threatened defendants.

Putting the shoe on the other foot, STAC Electronics used patent litigation to force a deep pocket defendant (Microsoft) to buy STAC (the plaintiff patent owner) at a nice price.

Patent Choke Points

In a "patent-on-demand" directed patent development program, target high value patent choke points. That is:

1.   Patent only what you need.

2.   Patent your value added.

3.   Use a market-driven approach to find high value patent candidates in your organization. Take the top five of each of:

   -      Product marketing (patents that sizzle).

   -      Patent what you are branding.

   -      Sales: what features would your sales department like to have. (This is a

nice source of invention. Yes, sales-
men are often market-driven inventors.)

-    Customer support. (These are basi-
     cally the repairmen, however they can
     tell you where the product is failing
     and where it needs improvement.)

-    R and D (be careful, do not slide into
     technology-driven patenting).

-    Manufacturing.

-    Use "patenting mapping" to see where
     your industry is going, and then target
     you business plan accordingly, and
     patent the future "toll gates."

-    See your software people for new
     proprietary software that they are
     spending lots of money on, for infra-
     structure or otherwise, but not neces-
     sarily as product. If you pay for it,
     own the patents. Call this "patent min-
     ing" and your software budget is the
     motherlode.

     To make this work, you may need to change or
establish a patent process in-house. Too often the current
patent procedure involves individual inventors who have no
idea of what is patentable or valuable. Their patented

inventions are technology that they think is "cool." They did not write up a disclosure which is reviewed by a boss or a committee that is equally attuned to technology and business. In fact, the boss may be reluctant to get the technical people to spend any time in patenting (and thus remove themselves by a production project). The system needs to be re-engineered and it is critical what process and personnel are used for the disclosure and patent committee. CEO and Board support and communications is critical.

Joint venturing with plaintiff or defendant in threatened patent infringement litigation is another target in the choke point analysis. For example, see the Johnson and Johnson joint ventures with Guidant, regarding coronary artery stents, which settled their litigation. Also see the Chugai - Amgen joint venture in Europe regarding the EPO drug that resulted in a settlement of the Chugai v. Amgen litigation over the EPO drug patents. Here the patent holder plaintiff used the patent exposure to force the defendant to become plaintiff's distributor in a market new to plaintiff.

Regarding venture capital and investment bankers, they now are interested in analysis of patent developments in a particular area. See if an investment target has convergent or divergent patent portfolios. (That is, is an investment target patenting the same sort of inventions that the whole industry patents, or are they patenting something else to fill a hole in the industry's patent structure without competition?)

Proctor and Gamble has an interesting licensing approach to the patent portfolio. Their rule of thumb is to license all of their patents three to five years out. That is, they monopolize all of their patents for 3 to 5 years. After that, all are open to license to all competitors at reasonable rates. This gets P&G the market lead, and then allows them to keep it, because competitors tend not to try to invent around the P&G patents. Instead inventors put their patents and development activities in unrelated areas, because competitors know that they can simply license the P&G patents within a few years with no development cost. And even after licensing, P&G gets its 2% or so of the market gross everywhere. Also, this encourages P&G to develop second generation improvements within the 3 to 5 years time frame to continue the market edge.

Under the P&G rule, 3 years after the patent issued, if it is in a product, then you can license it. Or, 5 years after the patent issued, whether it ever got into a product or not, it is open to license.

Japan will be very good at these concepts using patent mapping, patent mining, invention-on-demand, inventing-around, and invention-just-in-time. These tools are perfect for identifying and patenting "picket fence" and "toll gate" patent strategies. This allows the Japanese to "own their future for a generation". It also perfectly fits into the Demming-Japan approach of continuous incremental im-provement, which tends to target second generation improve-ments, and product development, as opposed to fundamental new research.

12

Stock Price and the Measurement of Innovation and Branding, for Directors, Officers, and Investors

"Technology is a differentiator in every marketplace."
-John Reed, former Chairman of Citibank

"When in doubt, count."
-Charles Babbage, 1792 to 1871,
inventor of the digital computer

A driving component of market capitalization is the development and exploitation of intellectual property, sometimes called intellectual capital. Therefore, it is now necessary to develop standard parameters for measuring the development and exploitation of innovation and intellectual property (IP) to (1) evaluate the stock price of a company, and to make the buy-sell decision for that stock, (2) evaluate a company in comparison with competitors in the same industry, and (3) to set budget benchmarks and best practices for intellectual asset management. This is essential for the boards of directors and top officers to manage their companies. It is also essential for the investment community to establish stock prices and PE's, even for company's not thought of as tradition technology companies. For example, Citicorp (a bank and insurance company) is both a market leader in business method patents and high value trademarks, and also, recently, the largest market cap in the S&P 500.

These IP metrics may be particularly important for junior technology companies where traditional measures of value, such as price to earnings ratio or earnings per share are not applicable, since current earnings may be nonexistent or not predictive of immediately anticipated future earnings.

These metrics constitute the precise measurement of innovation and branding. This allows objective comparison with competitors in an industry, and the establishment of industry benchmarks for budgeting and scheduling.

Patents to Sales

Indicative of technology innovation, including software and business methods, is the number of patents issued in a year, divided by the dollar volume of sales in that year. That is:

$$\frac{P(Y)}{S(Y)}$$

A higher patent to sales ratio indicates more patent protection of markets and infrastructures, causing higher sales and margins.

Patent Applications to Sales

A related variable is the ratio of the number of patents applied for in a year divided by the dollar volume of sales in that year:

$$\frac{PA(Y)}{S(Y)}$$

A higher patent application to sales ratio indicates increased future protection of markets and infrastructure.

These ratios of patents per million dollars of sales indicate how aggressively a company is pursuing the philosophy of "patent what you sale, sell what (and how) you patent", for infrastructure, products and services. This establishes legitimate patent monopolies to increase sales, prices and margins. Higher ratios indicate higher market and infrastructure protection. Lower ratios indicate lower protection.

Patents to R&D Costs

Another interesting technology parameter is the ratio of patents (or patents applied for) in a year divided by the total research and development expenditures for that year:

$$\frac{P(Y)}{RD(Y)}$$

A higher ratio indicates a more productive R&D budget, or at least a better protected R&D budget. The patent ratio indicates the current status. The applications ratio indicates likely future status and current activity.

Patents to New Products

Another good parameter is the number of patents issued divided by the number of new products and services announced for that year.

$$\frac{P(Y)}{NP(Y)}$$

A higher ratio indicates better protection of new products and services with patents. A ratio of 1.00 or higher indicates that on average each new product to service announced is targeted for patent monopoly protection. A ratio of less than 1.00 indicates that on average at least some products and services are being announced that violate the principle of "patent what you sale, sale what you patent."

If the ratio of patents to new product and service announcements is less than 1.00, then this indicates that an individual analysis of each new product and service should be undertaken to identify unprotected products and services, to see if any protection can be obtained.

Software Patents to New Software Costs

In industries with proprietary software, and this is now most industries, an important statistic is the number of software ("business method") patents in the year divided by the amount spent for custom (not "off the shelf") software in that year:

$$\frac{SWP(Y)}{\$SW(Y)}$$

A higher ratio of software patents to software expenses shows better software protection and better software. Since software patents are available not only for software products that are sold, but also for software enabled services that are sold (where the software itself is not sold but constitutes infrastructure), and for software enabled infrastructure (also where the software is not sold but used for competitive advantage), this ratio indicates the degree of management competence in monopolizing the competitive advantage of its proprietary software systems, and the ability of management to develop proprietary software systems that give competitive advantage.

In other words, if you are buying software, then you must be doing it because of its beneficial impact in the marketplace. And if you are buying <u>custom</u> software, then you must be doing it because off-the-shelf software that provides the same service does not exist. And if this software is of use to you, then it is very likely also of use to your competitors. Therefore, this software, even if it is infrastructure and is not sold by you, is new and gives competitive advantage. Therefore, you should be obtaining software patents to monopolize this competitive advantage.

Trademarks to Sales

Similar statistics can be prepared for the degree of branding. That is, the number of trademark registrations in a fiscal year divided by the dollar volume of sales in a fiscal year, indicates the intensity of branding of sales.

$$\frac{TM(Y)}{S(Y)}$$

Trademarks to New Products

A similar ratio is trademark registrations in a fiscal year divided by the number of new product or service announcements.

$$\frac{TM(Y)}{NPA(Y)}$$

Trademarks to Advertising Costs

Perhaps an even more interesting statistic is the number of trademark registrations in a year divided by the dollar volume of advertising and marketing for that year. The higher this number is the more the advertising dollar is being invested in the development of proprietary branding. The lower this ratio is the more likely the marketing budget is being wasted without developing any cumulative branding property.

$$\frac{TM(Y)}{A(Y)}$$

Matrix Coverage Analysis

Specific patent and trademark coverage analysis may be done in a simple matrix form. In a technology context new products announced may be listed in chronological order on the vertical axis. The patent portfolio covering the various products may be listed on the horizontal axis according to the issue date. Patent applications pending may be listed in the order of the application date. Boxes in the resulting grid matrix may be checked off where applicable indicating which patents cover which new product.

This matrix highlights new products that fail to have any plan patent coverage, which may be a mistake. The same analysis may also highlight patents for which no products have been developed. (These patents that may be good licensing opportunities since they protect no proprietary product.) Coverage of a new product by pending applications may be superior to coverage by existing patents, since it indicates that the new products are the results of a newly developed technology, rather than merely continuing old established technology.

A similar matrix can be developed for new products on the vertical axis and trademarks on the horizontal axis. This may highlight new products that enjoy (or lack) trademark coverage, and highlight trademarks that may be discontinued or sold.

Stock Price and IP Metrics

In a given industry, comparative analysis of metrics among competitors, and metric averages for the industry, is an indicator of a long term health, future EPS growth, and stock price growth. Averages of key metrics for innovation and branding for an industry may indicate benchmarks and targets for that industry.

Study correlating long-term stock price performance in an industry with intellectual property (IP) metrics, shows that players with better IP metrics show better stock performance. Good IP metrics add shareholder value. Bad IP metrics indicate that the company has a fever.

After the IP coverage matrix analysis, it is useful to do a technology analysis of new products with patent coverage to see if the products are innovative leaps forward or just in old existing niches. This is not a brute quantitative metrics analysis, but a matter of judgement and analysis of individual markets and technology.

Quantitative metrics analysis is good for large companies with established income statements, or large corporations with dynamic markets. There are more data points with a lower beta in the data. For smaller and newer corporations, the individual technology and product coverage analysis may be more important, with fewer data points and higher beta in the metric data. However, many young tech companies have little or no earnings, so PE and EPS metrics are useless; therefore, IP metrics may be some of the only objective metrics available.

The quantitative metrics approach is for the Board of Directors and top officers to set budgets and schedules, and to establish a process for innovation patenting and branding. It is also for investment bankers and money managers to evaluate stocks.

The product and technology matrix analysis is more for a smaller companies, venture capitalists, IPO investment bankers, M&A, officers, and P&L managers of large corporations to make specific day-to-day decisions.

ROI for Patents: A Supply-Demand Analysis of the Impact of Patents on Markets

It is relatively straightforward to compute the profits and return on investment (ROI) for a patent, where the profits come from direct cash receipts, such as license royalties and infringement damage awards, less the out of pocket costs of a license and litigation enforcement program.

However, how is the ROI for a patent calculated, when the patent profit comes from the impact of the patent monopoly on the structure of the market, and not from license royalties or infringement awards? In the patent monopoly case, the value of the patent is determined by the impact on

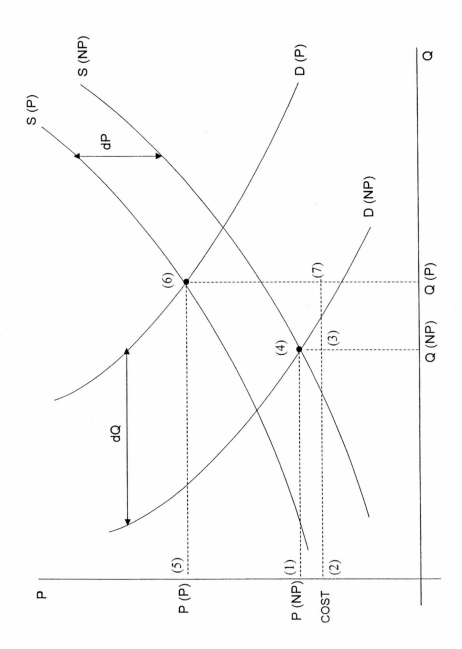

the market performance of the patented good or service. This value of the patent is equal to profit from sales (with the patent), less profit from sales (without the patent, that is with lower unit sales and lower unit price, caused by downward shifting supply and demand curves, caused by increased competition). This Patent Value, divided by the Cost of the patent, is the Patent ROI.

As shown in the accompanying Drawing, supply and demand curves for a market for a product or service with a patent would have the unit Price on the vertical axis, and the Quantity of units sold on the horizontal axis. The supply curve price would increase generally with increasing quantity. The entire supply curve with a patent S(P) would shift up, compared with the supply curve without a patent S(NP), because the patent would allow the supplier to charge a premium dP for each unit sold.

The demand curve price would decrease generally with increasing quantity. The entire demand curve with a patent D(P) would shift to the right, compared with the demand curve without a patent D(NP), because the patent would allow the supplier to be a sole source for the product or service, and the demand for a sole source would be higher, by dQ, at a given price than it would be at the same price were the product not sole source and in a competitive environment.

The Cost to supply each unit sold remains the same, with or without a patent.

At the point of intersection of the supply and demand curves, multiplying P(NP) x Q(NP) (price times quantity, no patent) yields the dollar volume of sales without patents. This is lower than P(P) x Q(P), that is, the dollar volume of sales with patents. The difference between these two revenue from sales, is the revenue added by the patent.

Subtracting the total cost to manufacture, that is Cost x Q, for the patent and no patent scenarios, yields the profit, with and without patents. That is, Profits (P) equals P(P) x Q(P), less Cost x Q(P), shown in the Drawing by the rectangle of points 2, 5, 6, and 7. And Profits (NP) equals P(NP) x Q(NP), less Cost x Q(NP), shown in the Drawing by the rectangle of points 1, 2, 3, and 4.

The difference between Profits (P) and Profits (NP) is the profit from the patent. Dividing this Patent Profit figure by the cost of the patent yields the profit margin on the patent, that is the ROI on the patent, resulting from the increased unit volume and unit price enabled by the patent monopoly. Summing the Patent Profit for all patents, and dividing by the total cost of the patent program, yields the profit margin, that is the ROI, for the entire patent program.

Where a patent monopoly is established in a market, the supply curve becomes unfettered in the upward direction, and the sole source supplier can set the price upwards where ever it may optimize his profits. That is, the patented supplier can freely set the price premium dP that he charges for his patented product or service. The patent protected supplier might best find this point of profit optimization by initially setting the unit price high, and then drifting it downwards to empirically find the point of profit maximization, while bringing additional capacity online.

This analysis of patent profits, where the profits come from increased market performance and not from license royalties and infringement litigation awards, is then similar to the supply-demand analysis of product differentiation and the resulting decrease in competition.

13

Patent Due Diligence for Technology Deals: How to Buy More for Less

Today, many technology deals are driven by patent positions, and evaluations of target companies are moved by patent due diligence. These technologies deals are to a large degree patent deals.

The Goals

The goal of patent due diligence in mergers and acquisitions, for the buyer, is to buy a better company at a lower price. The buyer should ask questions such as: Are the target's business plan and product protected from copying? Can the target practice its business plan without infringing the patents of others? How can patent problems that are identified be cured? Is a price adjustment necessary to deal with identified patent issues? What is the plan to increase share-holder value with patent strategies?

The goal of patent due diligence for the seller in mergers and acquisitions is to get the highest price possible and to close the deal. To do this, the seller needs to take the steps necessary to establish a investment grade patent portfolio (that is, a portfolio that would not prevent a deal from closing, and that will obtain a good evaluation). Because of the long lead times necessary to build a patent portfolio, this must be initiated before the closing, often years before the closing. This will then, at the time of the deal, satisfy the buyer that the buyer's due diligence issues have been properly addressed. Then in the deal phase, the seller should make a patent presentation to the buyer addressing and selling the fact of augmentation of shareholder value by the seller's patent strategy and patent portfolio.

A Competitive Advantage

A large competitive advantage can be had in the finance of technology companies by those who obtain access to patent professionals who can add value to a financial transaction. This is true for several reasons. Clearly, some large companies have sophisticated in-house professionals who fully understand their intellectual property and how to deal with it. But, most smaller companies cannot and do not have such talent on staff. Likewise, many operations that are financing technology companies, including some well known venture capital concerns, cannot and do not have the expertise to evaluate a patent portfolio, and its impact on a company. Furthermore, many patent law practitioners are not aggressive in pursuing these issues, for a variety of reasons, which may include legacy budget constraints, and narrow professional interests and training.

An Epidemic

Basic title problems are common in the patent world. But they can often be cured if acted on early enough. However, like badly poured concrete, the longer they sit, the harder it is to fix them. Ownership issues are the first thing to review in a patent portfolio.

Budget and Schedule

Almost no deal has a budget or schedule that will allow all possible patent due diligence to be done. The idea is do the basics, and then use judgment and some creativity to react to the basic results and to ascertain what else to do.

For example, validity opinions are rarely done during patent due diligence projects, because of the time and expense involved.

Five Fundamental Issues

Five fundamental patent issues in many deals are: 1) Are the target's products protected from copying by competitors, 2) Can the target make its product without infringing the patents of competitors, 3) Does the target own "its" patents and trade secrets, 4) What patent strategies will improve the shareholder value of the target going forward, 5) Do the price and terms of the acquisition need changing due to the answers to the above patent points, or are there other remedies for problems identified in the patent portfolio?

A Checklist: Seventeen Items

The following is a good minimum menu for more detailed patent due diligence. For any issues or problems that are identified, develop a plan to correct the same and close the deal.

(1) Properly identify all patents in the key transaction contracts, and use words of conveyance for these patents.

(2) Verify recorded assignments from all the inventors. <u>Identify any title defects and develop a plan to correct them</u>.

(3) Review all Patent Office filings and UCC filings for clouds on title.

(4) Include all foreign patents of interest.

(5) Review all licenses, partnership agreements, employment agreements, and other relevant contracts. Watch out for ownership "leaks" especially for "after developed" inventions.

(6) Ascertain if the target's products fall within the scope of their patents.

(7)   How secure are the target's trade secrets? Review its "confidentiality program."

(8)   Has the target patented its software or its services?

(9)   Review all the target's past attorney opinion letters regarding patents.

(10)   Review all past "cease and desist" letters regarding infringement, both sent and received. Query if laches have arisen. Is infringement willful? Is the target about to be sued?

(11)   Investigate the competition's patent portfolio, U.S. and foreign. Get your patent advisor to characterize the forest, not just the trees. Where is the industry going, and how does the target fit in? Can the target practice its business plan without being blocked by the patents of competitors? Can problem patents be licensed, cross-licensed, or invented around? Can the target protect its new products and services with patents from being copied by competitors?

(12)   Get representations and warranties from the target, and its patent counsel, regarding all of the above.

(13)   Once you have done the above, step back and decide what else should be done in this partic-

ular case, within the current schedule and budget. <u>Make a patent plan to improve the value of the target</u> . For example, can the target "invent around" its competition's patents? Can the target "invent-on-demand," or "invent-just-in-time," to evolve its currently unpatented products into new patentable variations?

(14)   Remember, <u>if you cannot cure a problem any other way, you can always change the price in the deal</u>, set up escrows and offsets securing representations and warranties, or ultimately (and this is the fire escape of last resort) you can just not close. Litigation, of course, is not generally considered to be a business transaction, and is best avoided.

(15)   Verify ownership of any overlapping, related, necessary or convenient patents, copyrights, or trade secrets, embodied in any proprietary software or other products or services.

(16)   Is a confidentiality program in place, to capture and own intellectual property that is being developed by the target, before the property is lost to competitors, employees, vendors, or the public?

(17)   Can the patent position of the target be used to enhance the target's revenues by licensing

non-competitors, or by enforcement action against infringing competitors?

Timing of the Patent Due Diligence Process

The earlier that patent due diligence is begun in the mergers and acquisitions process, the more valuable it is.

The buyer may begin patent due diligence in the target identification and the evaluation phase, prior to negotiation of the terms of the deal.

The seller needs to begin the patent due diligence process at the original business plan stage, when the seller is beginning its business, in order to eventually sell a company with maximum value, with an investment grade patent portfolio. The seller must begin its due diligence earlier than the buyer because it takes material lead time to build a patent portfolio, and because the option to apply for patents may be lost if applications are not made before the non-confidential commercialization process is begun for a new product or service. (However, in some lucky cases, a patent portfolio of value may be purchased from third parties relatively quickly.)

14

Responding to the New Demand Letters Alleging Infringement of Business Method and Software Patents

A new type of demand letter is now beginning to appear alleging infringement of business method and software patents. This is happening in industries that make extensive use of software but which in the past have not been exposed to patent strategies, such as financial services, telecom services, software, bricks and mortar retailing, and healthcare management.

(This chapter can be read in conjunction with Chapter 10, "Patent Litigation as a Business Tool", of *Patent Strate-*

gies for Business, third edition, a companion volume to the present book.)

These demand letters are often the prelude to eventual patent litigation (or licensing in a hostile environment in lieu of litigation), and therefore it is essential that proper and immediate responses be developed. Some commentators have suggested that receiving a demand letter is a bit like being bitten by a snake: whether you eventually live or die may depend on what you do in the first thirty minutes. This witticism is an exaggeration in the case of patent demand letters, but it does point out that these communications should not be ignored for long.

Some Background

In the 90's, the law was changed to make it clear that software is patentable subject matter. This led to a tidal wave of business method patent applications (which are better called "software" patent applications). For the first time, all companies with budgets for software and e-commerce had offensive opportunities for patent strategies, and defensive requirements for patent strategies, even where these patents were unrelated to products that the companies sold.

In the case of financial and telecom services, some of these business method or software patents directly impact services that were sold. In the case of software companies, the software patents sometimes directly affect the software products that were sold. However, for perhaps a majority of owners of business method patents, these patents affect the software infrastructure of the company and have more to do with how business is done than what is sold.

These patents are directed towards proprietary software of all types, including administrative systems, Internet architectures, e-commerce platforms, web pages themselves, and special new data structures such as data warehouses. Many of these patents do not directly identify goods and services that are sold, but intend to monopolize new infrastructure that provides a competitive advantage in "how" the business is delivered. Some of these business method patents protect new investment contracts, securities, and other methods of doing business that may not require software.

This change in law did not require a statutory change by Congress, but comprised merely case law application of established patent law principles, applied to new technology and fact situations.

These new facts were coming out of the explosion of software applications in business, the pervasiveness of the PC, the practical applications of the Internet, and the deregulation and technology changes in particular industries, such as financial services, telecom services, and retailing. In many cases, these patents also directly impacted the reorganization of corporate America along the lines of just-in-time manufacturing, just-in-time inventory control, flattening of the corporate organization chart, and elimination or compression of layers of the distribution chain for goods and services.

In effect, the old adage "patent what you sell, and sell what you patent", expanded to include "patent how you sell, and sell how you patented."

Leading cases of interest in this development include *Arrhythmia Research Technology, Inc. v. Corazonix Corporation*, 958 F.2d 1053 (Fed. Cir. 1992), *In re Alappat*, 33 F.3d 1526 (Fed. Cir. 1994 en banc), *Paine Webber v. Merrill Lynch*, 564 F. Supp. 1358 (Fed. Dist. Ct., Delaware 1983), *State Street Bank v. Signature Financial*, 149 F.3d 1368 (Fed. Cir. 1998), and *AT&T v. Excel*, 172 F.3d 1352 (Fed. Cir. 1999).

Demand Letters from Corporate Patent Holders

In the later 90's, a tidal wave of issued U.S. business method patents began to come out of the pipeline of applications at the Patent Office. Many of these went immediately to litigation and enforcement, presumably after a brief flurry of demand letter communication between the parties. In addition to the cases cited above, including *State Street Bank* (mutual funds) and *AT&T v. Excel* (telecom services), we saw *Priceline.com v. Expedia, Inc. (Microsoft)* regarding reverse auctions on the Internet for travel arrangements, *Amazon.com v. Barnesandnoble.com* (regarding the one click button on web pages for e-tailers), and a wide variety of other litigation. This litigation can be typified by the fact that both the patent holder and the defendants were in business and competitors with each other.

Demand Letters by Non-Businesses

In addition to corporate demand letters regarding business method patents owned by operating business entities, an increased number of demand letters have also appeared from patent holders that are not actually using the inventions described in the patents. For example, the Lemelson Medical Foundation continues to pursue enforcement of the more than 600 patents of Jerome Lemelson, including currently the machine vision and barcode patents involving laser scanners.

Also, Ronald Katz Technology Licensing LP has been pursuing the patents of Ronald Katz, regarding telephone call service centers and voice response units.

In addition, we have seen allegations, and in some cases litigation, regarding the secure encrypted Internet communication patents of Leon Stambler, and a flurry of patents in 1999 regarding "solutions" to the Y2K "problem".

Katz Patents

The Katz situation has reached an interesting stage. The Katz patents include approximately 50 issued U.S. patents, with about 2,000 claims. These arise from a small number of patent applications filed in the mid-80's, and in some cases result from tenth generation continuation and continuation in part applications based on those original parents. In the 90's, Katz pursued litigation in three cases against smaller parties in the telecommunications field. Two of these cases were settled and one resulted in a permanent injunction against the defendant, a little known company. In

1998, Katz LP and its licensee MCI were co-plaintiffs in a patent enforcement action against AT&T. In January 2001, after discovery and trial through a ruling in the Markman hearing (to interpret the scope of the claims of the patents at issue for purposes of the litigation), the case was settled. The terms of the settlement are secret but it is suggested by some commentators that AT&T made a large cash payment to Katz LP in settlement. After this settlement, Katz LP increased the pressure on banks, financial service providers, and telecom service providers to license its portfolio or face enforcement litigation. Apparently, Katz demand letters are currently circulating in these industries.

Lemelson Patents

The Lemelson situation is also interesting. In the early 90's, Lemelson litigated his bar-coding machine patents. In the later 90's, a wide variety of major corporations licensed the barcode patents from the Lemelson Foundation without litigation. Licensing, not litigation, became the dominant response to a Lemelson demand. The exact numbers are unknown, but some commentators have suggested that the Lemelson Foundation has receipts in excess of $1 billion from this license effort.

However, in the year 2000, the license trend was broken. This happened when approximately 60 members of the National Retailers Foundation determined to defend their use of mass market laser scanners at retail points of sale, without paying a license royalty to the Lemelson Foundation for the patents in question. This litigation is in its early stages and cannot be predicted at this time; however, the National

Retailers have filed an amicus brief attacking the validity of the Lemelson machine vision patents in a co-pending case.

How to Respond to the Business Method Demand Letter

There are several possible ways to respond to demand letters for business method patents. Some of these response options are particular to business method patents, and some apply to demand letters for all patents, and indeed for other intellectual property such as trademarks, copyrights, and domain name registrations. Some of the comments are also particular to patent portfolios that are owned by non-operating entities, whereas others are more particularly addressed to patent holders that are active business competitors of the addressee.

1. *Declaratory Judgment.* Some demand letters directly allege patent infringement for indicated claims of specific patents. These letters may give grounds for the recipient to affirmatively file a court action for declaratory judgment to invalidate the patents. This may allow the recipient of the letter to pick a beneficial forum and timing for litigation, such as in the "rocket docket" in Virginia.

2. *Opinion Letters Cut Exposure.* Being put on notice of possible infringement regarding patents, or even being put on notice of the existence of specific patents, may activate an affirmative duty of care to avoid infringement. This might require either seeking an opinion letter of outside counsel of non-infringement or invalidity of the patents in question, or seeking a license from the patent holder, or doing what is necessary to alter practice to avoid infringement in the

future. Failure to obtain such an opinion letter, or otherwise act, may enable triple damages in the event that infringement is eventually found. Such opinion letters may only be thought of as insurance against triple damages, however. Such letters do not directly impact litigation of issues of infringement, or of consequential single damages and injunctions. The opinion letter review process, even when ultimately an opinion letter cannot be given, may also serve to terminate infringement where it is found for a valid patent.

3. *License v. Litigation*. In situations where a license is being offered, the basic economic analysis is to compare the general alternatives of license (and its cost) versus litigation in the absence of a license (and its eventual cost and consequences). This views the license offer letter, and the demand letter, as at best "pre-litigation" situations. To look at it another way, the eventual patent enforcement litigation, or the threat of the same, is a step in the larger evaluation process to determine the eventual cost of a license settlement. (Surveys indicate that 90% or more of patent litigation between commercial entities end in settlement prior to a final non-appealable judgment in litigation.)

The license versus litigation choice is not digital. That is, license negotiations and litigation can run in parallel, and the course of each can profoundly affect the other. Of course, a decision to take a license (that is, to determine that the license is a "good deal", comparatively) can be made only by comparing the license to the expected cost of litigation. Hence, an analysis of possible litigation outcomes is required by a license offer. This litigation analysis also amounts to preparation for litigation, which may itself cause the patent holder to lower his offered license costs.

The question of evaluating a potential threatened patent portfolio can be quite complex. The effort can be time consuming, expensive, and unsure in its results. Some "patent terrorists", who are not business competitors and do not seek injunctions, but instead only seek license fees, are quite adept at offering license settlements in lieu of litigation, for one-time up-front cash payments that make the license look cheaper and more secure than the cost of litigation. This may be the case even where the patents in question may be invalid. (Note that all issued U.S. patents have a statutory presumption of validity, and the burden of proof on showing invalidity lies on the would-be defendant. This invalidation result can be pursued in federal court litigation, and the price tag is generally material, and the outcome problematic. In this environment, even a six figure cash payment may look like a cheaper alternative to avoiding even an invalid patent, when the patent holder appears to be in an economic position to finance litigation.)

In situations where large patent portfolios are being asserted, such as in the Katz or Lemelson situations, there may be an incentive to find outside counsel that are familiar with the patent portfolios in question, and who may have negotiated settlements with the patent owners before. This might expedite the outside counsel learning curve on complex patent portfolio evaluation questions, and obtain superior results in any settlement license negotiation.

4. *Chips for a Non-Cash Settlement.* One classic settlement scenario in patent infringement cases arises when competitors with large patent portfolios are involved. In such cases, each player may share some exposure to the patent portfolio of the other player. This exposure may serve as a deterrent to avoid litigation. However, where the situation melts down and results in litigation, each party can expect the defendant to respond with their own counter-claims of infringement. At that point, a classic settlement option may be a cross license of the respective portfolios to the respective parties, with little or no cash changing hands.

However, to play this deterrent and cross license settlement game, each player must have "chips" in the game. That is, each player must have their own patent portfolio to offer for cross license and to expose the other party to risk. Consequently, when one or more major players in an industry initiate business method or software patent strategies and start developing serious patent portfolios, it may be incumbent (if only as a defensive measure) on other major players in the field to pursue the same strategy.

This is interesting, for example, in the world of banking where the Citibank group has in the neighborhood of 70 to 80 business method patents, some of which are quite interesting, whereas most other major bank players at this time have little or no patent portfolio for business methods. We can expect this imbalance to rectify itself as other major banking players begin to activate patent strategies for themselves.

5.   *Invent Around.* In some cases, to avoid future infringement, invent around or invent on demand strategies may be available. This calls for a party to modify or tweak its business methods to decrease or eliminate its exposure to patent infringement claims. Because of the very plastic and rapidly adaptable nature of software, inventing around or invention on demand in response to demand letter allegations may be a more viable alternative for business methods and software, than in certain other technologies such as pharmaceuticals or chemical catalysts.

Intellectual Property and the Board of Directors

With large multimillion dollar settlements and judgments appearing now in intellectual property, and with companies being exposed to permanent injunctions to remove themselves from major lines of business and investments in infrastructure, the questions of intellectual property litigation and development of business method patent portfolios are now matters of a magnitude big enough to be dealt with by boards of directors and CEO's. Indeed, inaction at the highest level of corporations in the development and protection of intellectual property may expose officers and directors to personal liability for infringement, and waste of corporate assets, where inaction may prevent them from accessing the defense of the "business judgment rule". A patent strategy fitted to the corporate business plan, instituted at the highest level, is now necessary for offensive and defensive goals, and to deal with cease and desist letter "fire drills" being forced onto businesses today.

Also, it has become clear that for a successful intellectual property development program to be implemented in an
organization, it is necessary for this program to be supported
from the very top of the organization, in the business plan and
budget. Also, for intellectual property development programs
to be most effective, they should tie in directly with the
business plan and business development strategies of the
corporation, which emanate from the officers and directors of
the corporation. Increasingly, the board and the officers have
come to include individuals or committees charged with
direct responsibility for overseeing the development of
business method patent portfolios, intellectual property, and
e-commerce initiatives. They may also become involved in
an ongoing "patent survey" process (sometimes called a
patent inventory or patent audit process), that is, a matter of
minding the intellectual property stream being generated by
a corporation in its normal course of business, to develop the
intellectual property rights necessary to own the innovations
that the corporation is developing.

15

Portfolio Theory and Classes of Patent Holders: Responding to Patent Infringement Demand Letters

Disputes regarding allegations of patent infringement often begin with the patent holder sending a "demand letter" or a "cease and desist letter" to the alleged infringer. The letter usually puts the recipient on notice of the subject patents, alleges or suggests infringement, and may explicitly or by implication include both an offer to negotiate a pre-litigation license in settlement of the issues and a threat of litigation if a settlement is not reached.

(This chapter can be read in conjunction with Chapter 10, "Patent Litigation as a Business Tool", of *Patent Strategies for Business, third edition*, a companion volume to the present book.)

This presents the recipient with the high value issue of how to respond to the letter, and there are a spectacular array of possible response strategies for the recipient. The issues often reach "death threat" levels of importance for the recipient and require board of directors approval.

How to Respond? Look at the Sender

Certain broad principles of portfolio theory may be applied to the analysis of patent holders and patent portfolios when structuring response strategies for patent infringement demand letters.

Portfolio investment theory sees that the investment universe contains a wide variety of investment opportunities. The theory holds that an investment portfolio should contain a diversified mix of these investments, with each class of investment handled in its own way, so as to balance the risks and rewards.

Applying this approach to patents, we see that the universe of patent holders asserting patent claims in demand letters is diverse, with each type of patent holder presenting its own particular risks, strengths, and weaknesses. Therefore, each type of patent holder is best responded to in a different manner, and no two patent demand letters should be responded to in exactly the same way. Indeed, demands by different classes of patent holders may best receive different responses, even where the subject patent portfolios are themselves comparable.

Six Factors

Responses will vary according to the risks associated with each class of patent holder, the potential costs and benefits of dealing with each class, and the balance of risks and rewards. These considerations are in turn imported by the relative resources and goals of the patent holder and the recipient of the demand.

Different key characteristics upon which patent holders may be measured include:

1. Are they competitors or non-competitors?

2. Are they large corporate entities, or small corporate entities, or individuals?

3. Are they wealthy or not wealthy?

4. Are the asserted patent portfolios strong patents or weak patents?

5. Are the asserted patents broad patents or narrow patents?

6. Do the evaluators suggest strong infringement or weak infringement, or no infringement, by the recipient of the demand?

Large Competitor or Small Non-Competitor

The goals of the different classes of patent holders differ and the means that they have available to force the achievement of their goals vary. For example, a large competitor patent holder may seek only injunctions and damages; patent licenses may not be available. Conversely, a small competitor or a noncompetitor may seek to settle with a license and some sort of joint exploitation agreement, and be interested in only the occasional injunction to add credibility to their license program.

Other Species of Patent Holders

Foreign competitors attempting to enter the U.S. market may be more inclined to seek joint exploitation settlements, using an infringer as a U.S. distributor.

Under-financed patent holders may seek to settle, since financing enforcement litigation to conclusion not may be practical for them. They also may be more inclined to sell their patent properties to a large well-financed third party competitor who can undertake enforcement on their own account.

"Patent pirates," as they are often called by some commentators, who develop and attempt to enforce patents, but who are not anyone's competitors or even in business (other than the patent enforcement business), tend to fall into two classes. There is a relatively small number that have the financial resources to pursue enforcement litigation. Most famously in this category currently may be the Lemelson

Medical Foundation, and Ronald L. Katz Technology Licensing LLP.

There is an increasing group of small under-financed patent holders that are associated with plaintiff patent contingency lawyers, and independent patent businesses. These patent businesses are financed and in the business of acquiring infringed patents for under-financed parties, strictly for the purposes of licensing and enforcement. There is also a growing plaintiff's patent contingency bar in the United States, that is paralleling the earlier development of personal injury contingency plaintiff's lawyers, and antitrust contingency lawyers. The rule appears to be that wherever there are the possibilities of triple damages, punitive damages, or otherwise large judgments obtainable from deep pockets by under-financed plaintiffs, then a contingency plaintiff's bar will arise.

Different Responses for Different Types of Patent Holders

Different combinations of the key patent holder characteristics suggest different responses to their demand letters. For example, in the case of under-financed patent holders, or patent holders with weak patents, the value of the "stone wall" response increases. That is, if the plaintiff is less able to finance litigation, it may be productive for the defendant to increase the cost of litigation and refuse settlement.

In the case where there are weak legal positions for the asserted patents, then the value of counterattack may increase. Of particular interest is a counterattack that may involve invalidity or unenforceability of the plaintiff's patents, since this would not only shelter the defendant from liability, but would also threaten to effectively cancel the plaintiff's patents at suit and may remove plaintiff from the patent business.

In situations where inventing around is an option, this approach would make it easier for the defendant to stonewall plaintiff and refuse to settle, since the value of any eventual injunction would be minimal.

In the case of well financed patent holders with strong patent positions, an early settlement strategy may be most advantageous to the defendant, where reasonable settlement terms are obtainable. Particularly this may be so if early settlement may result in a discount.

The overall conclusion that can be drawn is that not all patent infringement demand letter situations are the same. Different circumstances may require radically different approaches by the recipient. Some might be best responded to by early and vigorous attempts to settle with the patent holder prior to litigation. Others might best be responded to by a complete refusal to deal with or communicate with the patent holder and a vigorous aggressive defense should litigation be initiated. This "stonewall" might be accompanied by protective opinion letters from counsel upon receipt of the demand letter, design around activities, and the preparation of affirmative defenses that may lead to invalidity and unenforceability of the patent. This approach may also lead to early declaratory judgment or summary judgment activities against the patent holder, initiation of reexamination activities in the Patent Office, and extensive and expensive discovery demands on the plaintiff, should litigation be initiated.

Where settlements are negotiated, some settlements might best be structured by defendant as a license, where others might best be structured as a joint venture involving distributorships by the defendant.

16

e-Patents for Internet and Banking Services: The Survey

In January of 2004, we updated our survey of U.S. banking e-patents and U.S. Internet e-patents. These are, generally speaking, a species of software patents, that is, "business method" patents. The primary finding of the survey is that the numbers of both banking and Internet e-patents are growing at an exponential rate. This explosive growth continued the trends established by our January 1999 survey (see Chapter 4of *E-Patent Strategies*, a companion volume to this book), and our June 1997 survey (see Chapter 30 of *Patent Strategies for Business, third edition*, also a companion volume to this book).

These patent portfolios are beginning to be enforced by litigation in the financial industry, and are just beginning to cause a revolution in how innovative financial business is conducted.

Banks as Owners

607 patents were owned of record by banks, up from 390 in the 1999 survey. Most of these bank owned patents cover software systems for bank services and systems. These included credit reports, smart card security, the monitoring of fund floats, checking systems, document image storage recognition and analysis, electronic funds transfer instruments, holographic check authentication, fail safe on-line financial systems, automatic teller machine systems, anti-counterfeiting laminated currency, remote banking, home banking, smart cards, and others.

An increasing number of these financial patents cover new forms of investment securities, such as mutual funds, derivatives, and debt. This is a revolutionary change in how financial innovation is brought to market, and substantially increases the rewards for creating new financial products.

Banking and Computer Subject Matter

Further, it is noted that the number of patents that dealt with subject matter involving computer applications in banking, regardless of ownership, was 4075, up from 510 in the 1999 survey. This with the above information about bank ownership indicates that a wide variety of computer and software applications for banking are not owned by the banks that are constrained by them. This may indicate that banks should become more aggressive in owning patents for the new products and systems that they themselves develop and use, rather than let others (particularly vendors and consultants) monopolize this market and its profits.

Banking and the Internet

Also, it is particularly interesting that the number of patents involving banking and the Internet, regardless of ownership, numbered 1309, up from 22 in 1999 survey. Note also that the first of these was not issued until November 25, 1997. We can expect that many more applications with this subject matter, banking and the Internet, are pending.

Home Banking

459 patents are indicated for home banking or remote banking subject matter, up from 33 in the 1999 survey. This indicates explosive growth in this area. The home banking and remote banking patents tend to refer to software and computer systems for their implementation.

The Internet

39,607 patents involve Internet applications, up from 609 in the 1999 survey. This is a stunning statistic and represents a 6500% increase over only 5 years. (And more are coming. Indeed, 65,190 pending Internet patent applications were published in the last two years, and no one knows how many unpublished Internet patent applications are also pending.)

Furthermore, the patent litigation shootout for market share for new Internet based products and services has begun. With all this new patent ammunition coming on stream, it is inevitable that the litigation shootout for market share will continue to grow.

Smart Cards

5153 patents are indicated for smart card subject matter, up from 322 in the 1999 survey.

This indicates an explosive growth in the number of smart card patents, and guarantees that an even larger number are pending in the pipeline at the Patent Office.

The Uneven Response

The two leading cases establishing patentability for software patents for financial services are *Paine, Webber, Jackson & Curtis, Inc. v. Merrill, Lynch, Pierce, Fenner & Smith, Inc.* 564 F.Supp. 1358, 218 U.S.P.Q. 212 (D. Del. 1983), and *State Street Bank & Trust Co.* v. *Signature Financial Group, Inc.* 149 F.3d 1368, 47 U.S.P.Q. 2d 1596 (Fed. Cir. 1998). In both these cases, the defendants bet against financial patents, and lost money when the patents were supported.

In this light, it is interesting that some financial players have yet to be indicated as owning any patents. (Some dogs appear to learn new tricks slower than others.) This is despite the fact that an increasing number of competing financial institutions have already committed themselves to the new opportunities available in financial patents.

This patent imbalance will lead to a re-allocation of market share to the more nimble patent savvy players.

For a particular company, a more specific and detailed analysis can be executed for the patent developments in their field, both by subject matter and according to ownership by their key competitors. This would indicate the direction of the competitors' patent portfolio from which they can expect offensive action. This can also suggest holes in the investigating company's own patent development that should be filled with patenting activities and perhaps product development.

The analysis of this survey covered only the U.S. issued patent database. A more detailed specific company analysis might also include published U.S. and foreign patent applications (many U.S. patent applications are not published). Covering foreign published applications might give an advanced indication of patents that may appear on the scene in the U. S. at a later date, since many foreign applications are also filed in the U.S.

17

Rules of Virtual Genius: Software and Internet Update

> *"I don't invent anything, until <u>after</u> I find a customer to buy it."*
>
> *-Thomas Edison*

The rise of software patents (that is, e-patents, or business method patents) and their application to Internet services, software applications of all sorts, insurance and financial services, virtual retailing, and business plans, has led to an addition and update of the rules of virtual genius (about how to invent in a corporate environment), described in Chapters 2 and 3 of *Patent Strategies for Business, third edition*, the earlier companion volume of this book.

The following are the new additional rules for software and Internet invention, for profitable corporate activities.

Rule 13: Internet-ify

Apply the Internet and patent your applications. Call this "Internet-ification". Develop new services enabled by the Internet, or provide new platforms that use the Internet to enable your old established services that were not previously provided by the Internet.

When you take these steps you will likely find opportunities to deny your competition the right to copy your applications, or to reverse engineer them, during the term of any patent for your advances. The patent opportunities may extend to the software application, the service provided, the hardware and software platform that facilitates the service, or the GUI (Graphical User Interface) that is supported by the system.

A fertile area for this rule is telecommunication services and remote services. For example, where previously a leased private telephone line may have been used as part of a system architecture, for example for a wide area network, replace that private telecom line with the Internet. This indeed has been the essence of the rise of VPNs (virtual private networks) that have replaced many older WAN architectures.

Rule 11: For Software Only -- 1999 Expansions

Rule 11 was first discussed in Chapter 2 of *Patent Strategies for Business, third edition*, the companion volume of this book. Rule 11 is expanded here.

Rule 11a: Find New Functions

Anytime you develop a new function that is facilitated by software, evaluate the possibility of patenting the software system delivering that function, to prevent your competitors from reverse engineering and competing with you in supplying that function. This is true for any software system. (See for example, the Stac Electronics Inc. Stacker data compression product, or spreadsheet software, or virtual bookstores on the Internet). A particularly fertile area to find new patentable functions are in the classic service industries such as telecom services, financial services, insurance, retail sales, and the newer Internet services.

Rule 11b: Assemble New Combinations of Old Functions, Provided by Software

It is an old principle of patent law, which was originally developed for the mechanical arts, that a "new combination of old parts" can be patentable in itself. One example of this may be the Wright brothers airplane. This was a mechanical invention that basically assembled a pre-existing German glider design, with the internal combustion engine (which was not developed by the Wright brothers), with a propeller or "air screw" (which was not developed by the Wright brothers, but was refined by the Wright brothers for the airplane). The resulting new combination with mostly old parts resulted in a fundamentally new invention with unprecedented results, that is, a heavier than air flying machine.

Now with the advent of software inventions, we have an analogous role for the "new combination of old functions".

These are sometimes called "Swiss army knife" inventions, since, like a Swiss army knife, they endeavor to find a new level of utility by creatively assembling a variety of different old functions or pieces into one product or platform. In the software area, it can be very useful and very "non-obvious" to invent efficient ways to bundle various functions that previously have been executed by incompatible software platforms, into one integrated system sharing common compatible databases. Facilitating this combination of functions often leads to a superior level of service, with reduced costs, and can represent an inventive step forward for society.

Rule 11c: Provide Old Software Functions with New Hardware/Software Infrastructures

Providing old functions and services with new and superior hardware/software platforms can provide great business opportunities and opportunities for patents. For example, see the replacement of pre-existing cellular analog phone systems by digital PCS mobile phones. Also, see the replacement of wide area networks on telephone leased lines by virtual private networks using encrypted communication over public and "free" Internet lines.

Rule 14: Develop a User Friendly (Intuitive) GUI, Patent It, and Make Sure it Downloads Quickly

Innovative GUI'S (Graphical User Interfaces) can be patented as virtual machines, much like the actual dedicated black boxes of an earlier generation were patented as actual machines or apparatuses. An intuitive, good looking, and fast downloading GUI can be an extremely valuable portal to any hardware/software system that provides useful services. As such, these GUI'S can be worth patenting, where possible.

Likewise, new GUI'S can offer opportunities for trademarks, copyrights, and design patents, which can all act together to help suppress copying of distinctive GUI'S by competitors.

Rule 12a: Mind the Aesthetics

Even in software and computers, minding the aesthetics is an important rule. Rule 14 discussed herein is partially an aesthetic application to GUI'S.

We have long advocated interesting aesthetic design for the PC industry. Particularly as the PC industry moves into "commodity" status, it will be a particularly useful if PCs junk their beige square boxes in favor of "packages" designed by, for example, any good Italian design firm in Milan. Examples of this approach most recently have been the Apple iMac, new Apple Macintoshes, and some Sun Microsystems products. This has brought both color and shape to the PC industry, finally, after two decades.

It typifies this trend, that Steven Jobs' first big success was creating the PC at Apple (it was an ugly little product that sold itself on function and price), while Mr. Job's latest success has been resurrecting Apple by putting the product in a pretty package (although it does the same old thing).

Swatch watches and Swatch cars have also brought aesthetics to products of industrial technology. The Swatch car uses interesting new design and manufacturing techniques to enable its eye catching design. Swatch watches, at least in the Swatch "Skin" line of watches, uses some modest new technology to make an eye catching fashion statement that is well evaluated in the marketplace.

Rule 15 (extension of Rule 5 -- Apply New Devices): Apply New Software Functions and Protocols

New functions are available from new software and they should be applied to your business wherever useful. These new applications to your business will, in turn, present opportunities for patenting the resulting new competitive advantages, in order to keep these advantages away from competitors. These new software functions include public key encryption, voice recognition, voice to text, text to voice, and hands-free interfaces facilitated by voice to text, to name a few.

Also, new protocols are allowing new levels of service at new lower price structures. These include the Internet 2 protocols, voice over IP, fax over IP, reserved bandwidth, real time IP (streaming format protocols), and VAN's (virtual private networks). These developments seem to apply as well to intranets as to the Internet.

Applications of extranets may also provide patentable competitive advantages. (Here we use extranet as a private system with a TCP/IP protocol, or a virtual private network, with some restricted partial level of public access). For example, this may include the ability of the public to access a web page and order products, in a system that will directly access and modify in-house inventory, shipping and receiving databases as a result of the order.

Rule 16 (an extension of Rule 5a - Apply New Devices): Apply New Digital Telecom Devices

PDA's (personal digital assistants) palm top computers, smart mobile phones (for example, with encryption and/or GPS), pagers with visual displays, PC digital cameras for the Internet, together with streaming video and audio over IP, cable modems, and PCS mobile phones (digital mobile phones), all are interesting new hardware features at reduced prices that have recently become realistic to incorporate into patentable hardware and software systems to deliver new services, or to deliver old services in new ways at new reduced prices. Consequently, these new applications present patentable opportunities.

Rule 17: Use Extranets and Artificial Intelligence to Eliminate Distribution Channels and Costs for Goods and Services

We have seen applications of this rule to books with Amazon.com, and to drugs with the affiliated Drugstore.com. We have also seen it in industrial hardware and in computers. See for example Dell Computer's web sales. We have seen it with financial services with Schwab and Fidelity's stock trading over the Internet. We have seen it with IPO's (a former principal of Hambrecht & Quist recently began to underwrite IPO'S on the Internet direct to retail investors in an auction system). We have seen it with goods and services of all kinds in Priceline.com. We have just begun to see it with life insurance (see the Schwab/Kemper life insurance quotes on the Internet). We have certainly seen it with the distribution of investment information and analysis for stocks and bonds over the Internet in a variety of locations (containing sophisticated charting and quantitative screening, and distribution of analytical reports). We have seen it with the new use of extranets which let vendors and suppliers into your transactional databases through the Internet and into your software for sales orders, accounts receivable, shipping and receiving and databases for the same.

Many of these developments when they were new offered opportunities for patented advantages in the marketplace. Some of the innovators were nimble enough to apply for patents (see Priceline.com) and some apparently were not (see Amazon.com).

For example, when the Internet bookstore idea was new, it probably presented a patentable opportunity, although apparently Amazon.com did not pursue this patent. If Amazon.com had obtained a patent for the virtual bookstore, Amazon.com would probably not now be in a brutal fight for market share (that is killing its profit margins) with Barnesandnoble.com.

On the other hand, we see Priceline.com obtained a patent on its business before its public roll out. (Although this patent may be litigated soon, and Priceline.com appears to have copycat competition, its eventual market share may be profoundly influenced by the success or failure of its patent strategy. And Priceline.com at least now has a shot at enforcing a patent home run. Amazon.com never gave itself even a shot at a patent home run, apparently.)

As distribution systems continue to be fundamentally reorganized by these Internet software systems (in industries such as insurance, financial services, and retail sales), the first player to implement new methods of increasing distribution and lowering costs should take any opportunities available to suppress copycat competition, to boost its market share and to maintain its margins over the long run. For these new Internet retailing applications ("e-tailing"), it remains to be seen where the profitable business model lies in the new compressed Internet distribution systems, without patent protection to eliminate profit margin competition.

My favorite example of Internet applications to retailing, which may not have been patentable at any time, is Fromages.com. This single web page has allowed one cheese shop somewhere in France to distribute its products by air courier throughout the world. This is particularly interesting to the U.S. cheese market, where unpasteurized French cheese processes cannot legally be used to manufacture cheeses, and where unpasteurized French cheeses can be imported only for personal consumption and not for resale. Only by direct retailing from France can these extraordinary cheeses be eaten in America.

Rule 18: Incorporate Remote Payment

Incorporating remote payment into your software-based remote sales system, whether it is by the Internet or other telecommunication means, provides opportunities to obtain a legitimate patent monopoly in new market areas. These opportunities include all areas of e-commerce, web credit card transaction authorization, smart cards, e-money, remote checking, and e-billing. Both these services and the software/hardware infrastructure for providing the services may represent patentable opportunities. Incorporating these methods into any business system can be opportunities of tremendous advantage.

Rule 19: Develop New Algorithms

Algorithms for software based decision making can be patentable in their own right. This could have a tremendous economic impact for a company that would be worth protecting. Older smart equipment and software, although it may function successfully, is today in retrospect not always as smart as it could be. Developing new decision making algorithms, whether they are quantitative and specific, or heuristic, or based on neural nets or other decision making algorithms, can dramatically improve the function of decision based software and smart equipment. This also applies to pattern recognition, image processing, and encryption software. It is also quite effective for the patent portfolio for the RSA Corporation, and their dual public key/private key encryption/decryption algorithms. It has also been used for program trading and other quantitative decision making. It has also been applied to a variety of smart equipment and expert systems by the telecom and defense industries; for example, see GPS based encryption algorithms, and the conversion of smart bombs from a laser guided targeting algorithm (which is susceptible to line of sight weather conditions) to GPS based target navigation with predetermined target coordinates (which works better in no visibility situations).

Rule 20: The Antidote to Inventing Around: Large Disclo-sure, Continued Prosecution, Late Claiming

A good procedure to use to inhibit competitors from inventing around your patents, centers on the idea of keeping prosecution of one of your early patent applications open with continuations and continuations-in-part (CIP's).

In this procedure, an initial early application is filed with the most extensive disclosure possible at the time. Additional matter is added in CIP's as developed. When claims are allowed, they are issued, but the application is kept alive with other claims, in continuations. When competitors appear, their products are targeted as well as possible with any available new "late claims" that are enabled by the original specification or early CIP's.

This is basically the Tollgate Strategy combined with the New Submarine Strategy. It is limited by the scope of the original enabling disclosure, and any early CIP's; but, it can ease the demands of completely inventing around yourself at the inception of your project, as an inoculation against your competitors inventing around you. (See Chapter 3 of *Patent Strategies for Business, third edition*, the earlier companion volume to this book, for a discussion of the antidote to invent-ing around, the Tollgate Strategy, and the New Submarine Strategy.)

18

Four Stages of Patent Denial in the Software Industry

Over the last few years, software patents have developed in the United States and their success in helping the bottom line for businesses that own software patents has been proven. This has caused many players in the software industry to go through levels of denial regarding software patents.

Stage 1: It's evil

Originally we saw many software professionals that were offended by the idea of software patents because of some sort of anarchistic or libertarian ideological impulse against change and development in this area. Basically, they thought that software patents simply "should not" be allowed. In some sense, software patents were seen as morally wrong.

This issue has now been decided by our society and software patents are here to stay. So the question now has become one not of what should be done for the good of society, but what must be done for the individual business to accommodate the circumstances as we find them. (The economic and social arguments in favor of patents in general apply to all new technologies, including software. However, this issue seems to be the subject of a fight we go through every time a fundamentally new technology is developed.)

Stage 2: It's the Market Share, Stupid

As it has become clear that software patents are here to stay, and whoever uses them has an opportunity to make a tremendous amount of money, the level of denial in the software industry against software patents has become more sophisticated, as it has eroded. As some software companies and owners of software applications are racing to the Patent Office to develop these software patent portfolios, others continue to hold back and be left behind with the argument that "it is not software patents that are important, it's the race to market share". That is, when a new product comes out, it is more important (the deniers say) to obtain market share; and market share is determined more quickly than it is possible to get patents out of the Patent Office. Then, by the time the patents are obtained, the original prior art is obsolete in the marketplace, the deniers assert.

There are several fallacies to this view. First, software patent applications can benefit from expedited review at the Patent Office and an accelerated issuance of patents.

The second and larger fallacy is that the determination of market share is, in the first years of a product, determined by market factors and probably not largely impacted by a portfolio of pending patent applications. However, the final determination of market share can be catastrophically, or triumphantly (depending on which side you are on) determined by a patent fight. This is because one of the results of patent infringement is not just an award for monetary damages for past infringement, but a permanent injunction for the life of the patent against the infringing party to no longer engage in the infringement. That is, the infringer may be put out of business entirely for the life of the patent. An example of this is the case of the *Stac Electronics v. Microsoft Corp.* (D.C. C. Cal CV-93-413-ER, May 13, 1994, June 8, 1994), about the original data compression product (which is discussed in more detail in *Patent Strategies for Business, third edition*, the companion volume to this book). In this case, Microsoft was found to infringe two software patents by Stac Electronics and as a result Microsoft suffered a permanent injunction. This may have reduced Microsoft's share of the data compression software market to 0%, regardless of whatever market share Microsoft had achieved by business means prior to the injunction. Perhaps, the only reason Microsoft Windows has a data compression feature today is that after the court defeat, Microsoft settled with Stac Electronics for an extremely expensive license to Stac's data compression software algorithms.

Hence, in the early stages of the development of a new industry, the race to market share is important and determined by business factors. However, once the market is developed, there is usually a shake out due to market forces. Then, the final market share allocation and market participant list is often determined by a patent fight. The essential lesson here is to position yourself to be a player in the eventual patent fight for market share. To do this, a company must very early in the development of the industry file its patent applications and obtain its early priority dates for those applications.

This scenario or general structure of development is a classic one for all new industries. It has been followed for data compression software in the *Stac Electronics v. Microsoft Corp.* litigation. It was also, in earlier days, followed for the wireless radio (Edison versus Marconi), for the airplane (the Wright brothers versus Glenn Curtis), for the automobile (Henry Ford versus everybody else), and for a variety of other industries created by Thomas Edison (who spent as much time in patent litigation as he did in the laboratory). Edison was quite successful in this endeavor and eventually ended up with significant earnings from major players in several industries that he initiated, including recorded music, motion pictures, radio, and electric power.

We are at the front end of seeing the same sort of patent struggle being played out in the final resolution of market share and profit margins in new software enabled markets. The litigation is just starting, but the major patent positions are currently being staked out with patent applications with today's priority dates.

Stage 3: It's Already Obsolete

A third state of denial for the software industry is that by the time the patents are obtained the products are obsolete.

What this actually means is that you may start your market with release 1.0, but by the time the patent issues, release 2.0 rules the market. The fallacy of this thought is that any patent filed immediately prior to the roll out of release 1.0, probably also controls the release 2.0 product. So, although release 1.0 may be obsolete in the marketplace by the time release 2.0 rolls out, the patent describing release 1.0 may still describe the fundamental core functions and software engine of release 2.0, and that first early stage patent may very well still prevent any effective competition to release 2.0. That is, although release 1.0 may still be obsolete, the patent for release 1.0 may still rule and dominate later improvement releases of the product in the marketplace. To put it another way, release 2.0 is probably a bells and whistles refinement to release 1.0, and these bells and whistles and improvements would be meaningless without the fundamental and patented inner core product. New functions of release 2.0 would be as meaningless without the underlying functions of release 1.0, as the top layer of the wedding cake would be without the underlying three layers of cake (it would look like Ken and Barbie standing on a cupcake).

Also note that the subsequent second generation improvements of release 2.0 can also be patented in their own right with second generation add on patents.

Stage 4: We'll Be Out by Then

Perhaps the most advanced stage of patent denial comes from some investors. Some short term investors, with an exit strategy to be out of the investment quickly, figure that by the time the patent shake-out comes to their market niche, they will have sold their position in the company. Therefore, they reason, it does not matter to them what the patent story is. The fallacy of this is that their sale price will in fact be profoundly influenced by the patent positioning of the company at the time of their sale. The value of Stac Electronics would have been about zero, if Stac had no patent to defend itself against Microsoft. But instead, Stac was evaluated at about $100 million, apparently, after it enforced its software patent (for an algorithm) against Microsoft. David can beat Goliath, and make a fortune, if David has a good patent in his sling.

19

Intellectual Property Surveys: Start with the Business Plan

Special Tips for Software, Telecom Services, and Financial Services

Elsewhere in the companion volume to this book, *Patent Strategies for Business, third edition,* we discuss in Chapter 1 an intellectual property strategic management program. We present here some additional ideas regarding intellectual property surveys (sometimes called intellectual property inventories or audits), particularly for software, telecom services and financial services. Note in particular that in these three fields, new services and new infrastructures for providing old services, are now candidates for patent protection. These developments are also candidates for infringement of the prior patents of others.

Start with the Business Plan

Intellectual property surveys should all start with your business plan. Only with knowledge of how your company plans to make money, can patent opportunities and threats be selected (or rejected) on the basis of what will most help your profits. This business driven approach is most clearly promoted by market-driven patenting, as discussed below.

Culture of Confidentiality

Probably the biggest change in software enabled service industries that are now entering the world of patents is the implementation of what I call a "culture of confidentiality". In particular, this requires all new product and service developments to be maintained as confidential trade secrets prior to their public roll outs. Also, the culture of confidentiality requires that any patent application be filed prior to the public disclosure of the trade secret. In addition, this culture of confidentiality requires a prophylactic title (ownership) regime as described below.

Prophylactic Title (Ownership) Regime

Contractual provisions and procedures must be put in place to avoid the pandemic title (ownership) defects that are common in the world of intellectual property today. Particularly, this requires all employees, consultants, vendors, potential customers, and other recipients of confidential disclosure, prior to the disclosure or their participation in the development of trade secrets and other intellectual property, to sign written agreements assigning all rights to the developments to the proper corporate entity.

These contracts are particularly easy to get many parties to sign prior to the development of the intellectual property in question, but can be quite difficult to arrange after such development has happened.

Also, note that normal business activity (absent these contractual agreements to cause title to come to rest in the proper place), may lead to title coming to rest in unintended and incorrect hands, with disastrous consequences to the proper corporate owner. Specifically, if patent applications are not filed early, then normal business activities to commercialize new developments may cause the ownership of the patent rights to the development to inadvertently lapse into the public domain, or worse yet, to unintentionally fall into the hands of an individual inventor on an exclusive basis.

Market Driven Patenting

The market driven approach to possible patenting requires that each new good or service that is contemplated be reviewed for patentability prior to its disclosure and roll out to the public. The patentability of software is not commonly understood by business and technical people in the software businesses, and is best appraised by a patent attorney familiar with software based patents.

Also, prior to rolling out new products or services, defensive patent analysis should be performed to ensure that the party developing the good or service has the right to sell the good or service without infringing on the prior patent rights of a competitor.

This is referred to as a "market driven" patenting approach because the protection of a previously defined market drives the push for patent weapons.

A larger view of market driven patenting involves an inspection of the business plan and methods by which the corporate client makes money. Then a creative search is made of possible patent opportunities to legitimately suppress competition and maintain profit margins for this plan. How this relates to planned new product roll outs is discussed above.

Regarding existing products and niches, the opportunity to patent the existing products may have passed if the products are already rolled out to the public. However, those old product niches may be placed into patent protection by the intentional development of second generation patentable improvements that will obsolesce prior non-patented products and services.

Sometimes, a good source of market driven patent ideas is the Marketing and Sales Department.

Technology Driven Patenting

The technology driven patenting process involves looking at the best new in-house ideas for products and services, whether or not they may be presented by the corporation to the marketplace, and protecting them with any available patent strategies. These patents may then be used to protect any eventual product roll out, or may be sold as assets to non-competing third parties if the corporation decides not to exploit these products and services itself.

This is called technology driven patenting because interesting technology (independent of any apparent markets) drives the push for patent property.

Legally Driven Patenting

Legally driven patenting may involve an inspection of the competition's products and services and their intellectual property position. Gaps in the competition's intellectual property protection may then be identified. The inspecting corporation may then invent into those patent gaps of the competition to attack the competition's products and markets with the inspecting corporation's own new patentable product improvements.

A second approach to legally driven patenting involves, first, research directed at the patented technology developments of the entire industry, conceptualization of the directions of development, and inventing into the future destination of industry development, possibly using a "submarine patent claims" approach and late claiming within 20 years of any original patent application date.

A third legally driven patenting approach would incorporate identification of a specific problem patent of a competitor that is blocking entry into a target product niche (i.e., identifying a potential patent infringement plaintiff/competitor), and then responding to the problem by "inventing around" the specific patent in question. This may allow entry into the product niche and attack on the target clients of the competitor, without exposure to infringement liability.

As a practical matter, a problem patent may identify itself. This can happen, for example, when (1) a company is sued for patent infringement, (2) a company receives a cease and desist letter, a cease and desist letter, or an offer to take a patent license (implying litigation in the alternative), or (3) a company is paying expensive royalties on an existing patent license.

Being sued for patent infringement is probably the most urgent incentive to legally-driven patenting, but inventing around is rarely actually done in response to litigation. This is because it is difficult to invent on demand, and because the patent bar traditionally does do value based compensation, instead of hourly compensation. Defendants would invent around plaintiffs' patents much more often, if only they could. However, in a few cases, inventing around plaintiff's patents has, when done, yielded huge returns by avoiding plaintiff's permanent injunction, while remaining in the marketplace.

We call this approach "legally-driven" patenting because it is driven by a need to improve the existing legal environment presented by the patent environment that a corporation must work in. This is an underdeveloped approach to patenting, but can give high returns. It has unusual demands for inventive patent lawyering, working closely with business and technical people.

Patent Profits

It is interesting that an increasing number of corporations in the U.S. have managed to make their patent portfolios become cash flowing profit centers. These may include, for example, Texas Instruments, IBM, Medtronic, Alza, and a variety of new privately-held start-up companies.

What used to be a headquarters staff overhead cost, that is patenting and licensing, is now budgeted as a profit center in more corporations. Although profits alone should not be the only goal of that function (some patents are best not licensed), positive cash flow certainly makes it easier to fund this operation in the annual budget.

20

Intellectual Property Surveys: Special Steps

The following is a list of specific steps that may be executed in an intellectual property survey (sometimes called an intellectual property inventory or audit). An intellectual property program may be developed with all these steps or selected steps that are most applicable to a specific company.

Industrial Intelligence and Response

An intellectual property survey may be used for legitimate industrial intelligence to determine what your major competitors are doing and to respond to the same before severe problems are generated for you by your competitors. The following steps may be followed:

Step 1:   List your major competitors.

Step 2:   Inventory the current U.S. and foreign patents issued to your major competitors. Also, search the published foreign patent applications of your competitors that have not yet resulted in patents in the United States.

Step 3:   Group the resulting inventory of competitor patents by product line and industry.

Step 4:   Characterize market niches and directions of the patent portfolios developing with your competitors.

Step 5:   Determine if "invent-around" opportunities exist for you for any particular patent grouping of your competitors. (Rules for inventing-around competitor patents are discussed elsewhere in Chapters 2 and 3 of *Patent Strategies for Business, third edition*, the earlier companion volume of this book.)

Step 6:   Determine whether you can use a leap frog and tollgate strategy for any group of competitor patents. (The leap frog strategy and tollgate strategy are discussed elsewhere in Chapters 2 and 3 of *Patent Strategies for Business, third edition*, the earlier companion volume of this book.)

Step 7:   Determine if any group of competitor patents blocks any of your planned products or lines of business. If so, develop an invent-around strategy for each of your blocked future products.

Step 8:   Plot the number of patents issued per year for each competitor and product grouping. From this determine the rate of growth of competitor patents in your industry. Use this percentage growth as a benchmark for your development of a patent portfolio for your own company.

Step 9:   Develop a list of key terms and key fields for patent developments in your industry.

Step 10:   From the list in Step 9, find the key patents in your industry, and determine who owns these key patents. Determine   invent-around strategy possibilities for such patents.

A Market Driven Intellectual Property Survey for Existing Products and Services

A market driven intellectual property survey process for existing lines of business may have the following steps.

Step 1: Inventory all the intellectual property in your company at this time. This includes patents, trademarks, copyrights, and trade secrets. The inventory should also include license agreements, joint development agreements, partnership agreements and other contractual arrangements that may impact intellectual property. These may include bringing intellectual property into your company, transferring out intellectual property from your company, and the development and ownership of intellectual property in the future.

Step 2: Inventory the major existing product or service lines of business of your company.

Step 3: Correlate your intellectual property with the products and services that are protected by the intellectual property. From the opposite point of view, also correlate your lines of business with the intellectual property protecting each line of business from avoidable competition.

Step 4: Determine if any of your products or services are unprotected from avoidable competition by intellectual property. If so, develop an intellectual property strategy to protect each unprotected line of business. Be sure to apply this process to new lines of business that are not yet for sale but planned and under development.

Benchmark 1

Each product should have at least one intellectual property protecting that product from competition. Utility patents, where they can be obtained, may be the best form of protection available.

Step 5: Plot the growth of your intellectual property, especially your patents, over time. As a bench mark, determine whether your rate of intellectual property portfolio growth is keeping up with that of your competitors.

Step 6: Determine the major lines of business of your competitors.

Step 7: Determine what intellectual property, if any, is protecting each of your competitor's lines of business.

Step 8: Develop a strategy to defeat any intellectual property protecting each of your competitor's lines of business from your competition. In the case of competitor patents, determine if they can be invented around.

Market Driven Intellectual Property Survey for New Products and Services

Step 1:   List all your   new   lines of business (goods or services) currently under development.

Step 2:   Itemize your intellectual property strategy for protecting each of these new lines of business from competition.

Step 3:   Determine the risk for each new line of business of suppression by competitors asserting infringement of competitors' intellectual property. Where the risks are serious, determine a strategy to legitimately circumvent the competitor's intellectual property.

Technology Driven Intellectual Property Survey

Step 1:   Inventory each research and development effort at your company.

Step 2:   Specify the intellectual property for each project under development, both offensive (to protect from copycat competition by competitors), and defensive (to avoid infringement attacks by your competitors enforcing their intellectual property).

Step 3:   For unprotected R&D projects, develop an adequate intellectual property strategy (offensive and defensive), or consider terminating the project. (Sell what you can patent, patent what you can sell.)

Benchmark 2 (For Manufacturing)

A rule of thumb in some manufacturing industries is to develop one patent for each $1 million of research and development funds expended.

Licensing

Step 1:   From your intellectual property inventory, determine which intellectual properties do not cover a current or planned line of business. Determine for each of these intellectual properties if you may sell or license that intellectual property to a non-competitor to generate cash flow.

Step 2:   Regarding each intellectual property that covers a current or planned good or service, determine if that intellectual property may be licensed on a non-exclusive basis for cash to use in a non-competitive way.

Patent Cluster Analysis

Step 1:   List your current patents.

Step 2:   Check the appropriate data bases to determine which of your patents are referred to as named prior art references in other patents. Develop a "lineage" chart of patent cross references to prior art.

Step 3:   Determine the owners of the various patents in the cross reference lineage chart.

Step 4:   Determine if any of your patents are developing a cluster of patents around them from a particular competitor referring to your individual patent. This may indicate that a competitor is attempting a "picket fence" strategy to contain the utility of one of your key patents. (The "picket fence" strategy is discussed elsewhere in Chapter 3 of *Patent Strategies for Business, third edition*, the earlier companion volume of this book).

Step 5:   If any of your key patents are being "picket fenced", determine if the competitor's picket fence patents can be "leap frogged". (The "leap frog strategy" is discussed elsewhere in Chapter 3 of *Patent Strategies for Business, third edition*, the earlier companion volume of this book.)

Step 6:   Determine if you can "picket fence" any of your competitor patents in your industry.

Appendix

Interesting Recent Cases

There are a great variety of very interesting current events in the world of patent development and enforcement. It is not possible to cover all these events here, but a few of the highlights are below.

Measure of Damages for Infringement

In August 1999, the Federal Circuit handed down what may prove to be a very influential case for all patent holders, *Grain Processing Corporation v. American Maize Products* 185 F. 3rd 1341 (Fed. Cir. 1999). Although this case is not immediately new, its application is a developing current event. This case held that a judicial finding that a non-infringing product or process existed and was "available" in the marketplace and acceptable to consumers precluded an infringement award for lost profits. However, the fact that the non-infringing product or non-infringing process was not actually sold in the market during the infringement period did not render the product as "unavailable", and the facts could still be used to preclude an award for lost profits. This case is increasingly used, where the facts support it, to mitigate the evaluation of damages where infringement has been found. Applying this case together with a successful design around effort to dodge the business impact of an injunction against future infringement, can do a lot to take the sting out of losing an infringement case for a defendant.

Patents as Collateral

On June 6, 2001, the Ninth Circuit handed down the decision in *In re Cybernetic Services Inc.* 252 F. 3d 1039 (9th Cir. 2001). This case held that filing a UCC-1 financing statement under the California State UCC regime establishes the priority of a security interest in patents that is senior to the priority of later filed security interests. No U.S. Patent and Trademark Office filing is needed for this priority.

The reasoning of the case may provide only a pyrrhic victory for lien holders of patents. The rationale of the case is that the federal patent statute does not address security interests and therefore does not preempt state law on that question. But, if one extends this line of reasoning, then the assignment obtained by a non-judicial foreclosure of such a security interest would not under the federal statute obtain the priority date of the foreclosed security interest. Hence, the foreclosure assignment would not cut off any intervening assignments to third parties, filed after the security interest was filed but prior to the foreclosure assignment filing. You might call this a 'Peter Pan' security interest, because it never 'grows up' to become a complete title to the patent, even after foreclosure.

Once again, this points out the failure of Congress to adequately amend the patent statute to deal with this situation. (A simple amendment to the federal statute that would take care of this circumstance was published in the earlier companion volume of this book, Patent Strategies for Business. Case law cannot adequately remedy the deficiencies of the federal patent statute. The incomplete federal statute fails to provide the enabling statutory basis for a reliable patent title search, and for patent title insurance.

The result of all of this is that the practical value of trillions of dollars intellectual property is minimized in the United States, and that the financing of technology companies is unnecessarily inhibited. For example, the ability of patents to be used in collateral based lending and structured finance would be dramatically improved if these statutory deficiencies were corrected. To date, the only secure way to "foreclose" on patent collateral is to put the borrower in bankruptcy and to obtain title from the bankruptcy judge as part of a judicially approved plan of reorganization.

To see how the federal patent statute should work, and could be written, there is a very interesting case that demonstrates how the analogous issue is properly handled for airplanes. See *Holiday Airline Corp. v. Pacific Propeller* 620 F.2d 731 (9th Cir. 1980).

Prosecution Latches

The principle of prosecution latches was affirmed in *Symbol Technology v. Lemelson Medical Foundation*, 277 F. 3d 1361 (Fed. Cir. 2002), *cert. denied* 537 U.S. 825 (2002).

In this case, the court applied the defense of prosecution latches against submarine patents. Prosecution latches is an equitable defense against enforcement of an otherwise valid patent based upon fundamental issues of fairness. The defense turns on the patent holder's unreasonable delay in seeking claims at the Patent Office to an invention, after an intervening public use or publication of the invention. The court confirmed that unreasonable delay after intervening public use or publication of the invention may result in the inventor losing patent rights to which the inventor may otherwise have been entitled. This directly attacks late claiming addressed to specific products in the marketplace for a long delayed submarine patent. This holding may dramatically reduce the value of the Lemelson patent portfolio, and may be used against other submarine patents. Although Lemelson is a so-called "patent pirate" (that is, one who has a large patent portfolio but is not in the business of making or selling the inventions in question), these same defenses may be used against corporate patent holders who are practicing their claimed inventions, if there are similar circumstances of submarine patents and late claiming after intervening public use or publication.

Patent Application as a Tort

In February 2002, the U.S. District Court Southern District of New York issued *In re Buspirone*, 211 F.R.D. 249 (SD NY, 2002). In this case, it was decided that a patent applicant may have antitrust liability to competitors where a patent application is made when the applicant knows that it has no valid grounds for obtaining a patent, and the applicant's intent in filing the application is to delay competitors in releasing a product on the marketplace. Although this case may have unusual facts and not be of common application, it does emphasize the principle that patent applications should be pursued, and patents enforced licensed and enforced, with at least a minimum standard of good faith and fair dealing, so as not to be construed as unfair business practice. Even though patents have a unique constitutional level of protection and exclusive monopoly-like benefits that they confer for a limited time (see the U.S. Constitution Article I, Section 8), it is possible in extreme cases to misuse this opportunity in a tortious manner. (Indeed, it is possible to abuse any other basic legal right, such as, for example, contract.)

Officer and Director Liability for Corporate Infringement

A recent case emphasizes the issue of potential personal liability of officers and directors for corporate patent infringement. See *Katz Technology Licensing, L.P. v. Verizon Communication, Inc.* 66 USPQ2d 1045 (E. D. Penn. 2002). This case holds "that piercing the corporate veil is not necessary to hold officers [and directors] of a corporation liable for patent infringement", even though "piercing the corporate veil is ... required to hold stockholders liable [for corporate patent infringement]".

This personal exposure of officers and directors for corporate patent infringement suggests the value of a patent committee of the board of directors, a CPO (Chief Patent Officer), an intellectual property holding company subsidiary, a patent profit center and business unit, and purchase of a patent infringement endorsement for the corporate errors and omissions insurance policy.

Patents and Shareholder Value

In the 90's, it became clear that intellectual property can add large increments to the shareholder value of companies. However, there has been much debate about how best to measure or assess this value. There is now a patent recently issued claiming an algorithm for evaluating companies and picking stocks based on quantitative analysis of their intellectual property portfolios. See U.S. Patent No. 6, 175, 824, issued January 16, 2001, for "method and apparatus for choosing a stock portfolio based on patent indicators". We certainly are not offering investment advise and have no comments on the possible utility of this patent's algorithm, but the effort clearly reflects the interest in the value of intellectual property and shareholder value. It is also a response to the inability of current accounting standards to report the true value of patent assets (instead of merely reporting their cost basis, which is virtually unrelated to market value).

This realization that intellectual property constitutes valuable property can also be seen manifested in two recent patent applications for novel securities, U.S. Patent Application No. 20030061064 for "capitalization of intellectual property", and U.S. Patent Application No. 20030138384 for "intellectual capital based venture investment". We cannot comment here on the possible merit of these particular developments, but we can certainly at least enjoy the irony of patents about patents.

Index

domain name: registration, 49-50; assignment, 50

due diligence: 1-3, 19, 21-23, 91; and industrial espionage, 5-7; checklist, 94-96; fundamentals, 93; in mergers and acquisitions, 91-94; timing, 96-97

Economic Espionage Act of 1966, 7

E-patents, survey of, 99-103

extranets, 111

Fromages.com, 113

Graphical User Interface (GUI): 106, 108; aesthetics, 109

home banking: number of patents, 101-02

industrial intelligence, 103, 131-33

infringement: 22, 85, 119, 127-28; of business method and software patents, 73

innovation protection, 55

intellectual property surveys: 123-29; benchmarking, 128; market driven, 133-34, 135-36; steps to, 131-38; technology driven, 136

intellectual property: as a source of income, 33; licensing, 57; metrics, 64, 70; new strategy, 55; old strategy, 55

internet patents, 102, 105-06

"invent around" strategy, 27-28, 81-82, 132-33

"invention on demand" strategy, 81-82

inventions: new combination of old functions, 107; Swiss army knife, 107-08

inventor and patent assignment, 17, 20

Jobs, Steven, 109

joint ventures, 58

"just in time": manufacturing, 75; inventory control, 75

Katz, Ronald, 76-77

Lemelson Medical Foundation: 76, 77-78, 80, 88

licensing: 77-78, 79,137; strategy of Proctor & Gamble, 61

litigation: 77-78; analysis of outcomes, 80

market capitalization, 63

MasterCard International, 100-01, 103

matrix coverage analysis, 68-69, 70

Microsoft Corp, 9-13, 119-20, 121

monetization, 33

National Retailers Foundation, 78

non-cash settlement, 81

patent application: abandonment, 37; examiner interview, 38;
    filing, 36-39

patent cluster analysis, 137-38

patent contingency lawyers, 88

patent leverage, 57-58

"patent mapping," 60

patent metrics: formulas, 64-67

"patent mining," 60

patent pirates, 88

patent portfolio development: expedited procedures, 35-39

patent portfolio: 20, 22, 86, 92; alternative uses for, 33; and
    ownership issues, 93; as profit centers, 128-29;
    legacy, 29

"patent terrorists," 80

Printed in the United States
43503LVS00004B/22-42